WRATH AND MERCY

INTERNATIONAL THEOLOGICAL COMMENTARY

George A. F. Knight and Fredrick Carlson Holmgren
General Editors

WRATH AND MERCY

A Commentary on the Books of
Habakkuk and Zephaniah

MÁRIA ESZENYEI SZÉLES

Translated by
GEORGE A. F. KNIGHT

WM. B. EERDMANS PUBL. CO., GRAND RAPIDS

THE HANDSEL PRESS LTD, EDINBURGH

First published 1987 by William B. Eerdmans Publishing Company,
255 Jefferson Ave. S.E., Grand Rapids, Michigan 49503
and
The Handsel Press Limited
33 Montgomery Street, Edinburgh EH7 5JX

Library of Congress Cataloging-in-Publication Data

Eszenyei Szeles, Maria.
Wrath and mercy : a commentary on the books of
Habakkuk and Zephaniah
Maria Eszenyei Szeles : translated by George A. F. Knight.

p. cm. — (International theological commentary)
Bibliography: p. 117
ISBN 0-8028-0242-7
1. Bible. O.T. Habakkuk — Commentaries. 2. Bible. O.T.
Zephaniah — Commentaries. I. Title. II. Series.
BS1635.3.E69 1987 224′.9507 — dc19 87-16771

Eerdmans ISBN 0-8028-0242-7

British Library Cataloguing in Publication Data

Szeles, Maria Eszenyei
Wrath and Mercy : a commentary on the books of Habakhuk and
Zephaniah. — (International theological commentary).
1. Bible. O.T. Habakhuk — Commentaries
2. Bible. O.T. Zephaniah — Commentaries
I. Title II. Series
224′.9507   BS1635

Handsel ISBN 0 905312 72 4

CONTENTS

ABBREVIATIONS

BHK	*Biblia Hebraica*, ed. R. Kittel
BHS	*Biblia Hebraica Stuttgartensia*
ca.	about
E	Elohist author/tradition in the Pentateuch
ed.	editor, edition
fem.	feminine
Heb.	Hebrew
LXX	Septuagint
mg	marginal note to the text of the RSV
MT	Masoretic Text (Hebrew)
NEB	New English Bible
NT	New Testament
OT	Old Testament
P	Priestly author/tradition in the Pentateuch
1QpHab	*Pesher* (commentary) on Habakkuk from Qumran Cave 1
RSV	Revised Standard Version
ZAW	*Zeitschrift für die alttestamentliche Wissenschaft*

EDITORS' PREFACE

The Old Testament alive in the Church: this is the goal of the *International Theological Commentary*. Arising out of changing, unsettled times, this Scripture speaks with an authentic voice to our own troubled world. It witnesses to God's ongoing purpose and to his caring presence in the universe without ignoring those experiences of life that cause one to question his existence and love. This commentary series is written by front-rank scholars who treasure the life of faith.

Addressed to ministers and Christian educators, the *International Theological Commentary* moves beyond the usual critical-historical approach to the Bible and offers a *theological* interpretation of the Hebrew text. Thus, engaging larger textual units of the biblical writings, the authors of these volumes assist the reader in the appreciation of the theology underlying the text as well as its place in the thought of the Hebrew Scriptures. But more, since the Bible is the book of the believing community, its text has acquired ever more meaning through an ongoing interpretation. This growth of interpretation may be found both within the Bible itself and in the continuing scholarship of the Church.

Contributors to the *International Theological Commentary* are Christians — persons who affirm the witness of the New Testament concerning Jesus Christ. For Christians, the Bible is *one* scripture containing the Old and New Testaments. For this reason, a commentary on the Old Testament may not ignore the second part of the canon, namely, the New Testament.

Since its beginning, the Church has recognized a special relationship between the two Testaments. But the precise character of this bond has been difficult to define. Thousands of books and articles have discussed the issue. The diversity of views represented in these publications makes us aware that the Church is not of one mind in expressing the "how" of this relationship. The authors of this commentary share a developing consensus that any serious explanation of the Old Testament's relationship to the New will uphold the integrity of the Old Testament. Even though Christianity is rooted in the soil of the Hebrew Scriptures, the biblical interpreter must take care lest he "christianize" these Scriptures.

Authors writing in this commentary will, no doubt, hold varied views concerning *how* the Old Testament relates to the New. No attempt has been made to dictate one viewpoint in this matter. With the whole Church, we are convinced that the relationship between the two Testaments is real and substantial. But we recognize also the diversity of opinions among Christian scholars when they attempt to articulate fully the nature of this relationship.

In addition to the Christian Church, there exists another people for whom the Old Testament is important, namely, the Jewish community. Both Jews and Christians claim the Hebrew Bible as Scripture. Jews believe that the basic teachings of this Scripture point toward, and are developed by, the Talmud, which assumed its present form about A.D. 500. On the other hand, Christians hold that the Old Testament finds its fulfillment in the New Testament. The Hebrew Bible, therefore, belongs to both the Church and the Synagogue.

Recent studies have demonstrated how profoundly early Christianity reflects a Jewish character. This fact is not surprising because the Christian movement arose out of the context of first-century Judaism. Further, Jesus himself was Jewish, as were the first Christians. It is to be expected, therefore, that Jewish and Christian interpretations of the Hebrew Bible will reveal similarities *and* disparities. Such is the case. The authors of the *International Theological Commentary* will refer to the various Jewish traditions that they consider important for an appreciation of the Old Testament text. Such references will enrich our understanding of certain biblical passages and, as an extra gift, offer us insight into the relationship of Judaism to early Christianity.

An important second aspect of the present series is its *international* character. In the past, Western church leaders were considered to be *the* leaders of the Church — at least by those living in the West! The theology and biblical exegesis done by these scholars dominated the thinking of the Church. Most commentaries were produced in the Western world and reflected the lifestyle, needs, and thoughts of its civilization. But the Christian Church is a worldwide community. People who belong to this universal Church reflect differing thoughts, needs, and lifestyles.

Today the fastest growing churches in the world are to be found, not in the West, but in Africa, Indonesia, South America, Korea, Taiwan, and elsewhere. By the end of this century, Christians in these areas will outnumber those who live in the West. In our age, especially, a commentary on the Bible must transcend the parochialism of Western civilization and be sensitive to issues that are the special problems of persons who live outside of the "Christian" West, issues such as race relations, personal survival and fulfillment, liberation, revolution, famine, tyranny, disease, war, the poor, religion and state. Inspired of God, the authors of the Old Testament knew what life is like on the edge of existence. They addressed themselves to everyday people who often faced more than everyday problems. Refusing to limit God to the "spiritual," they portrayed him as one who heard and knew the cries of people in pain (see Exod. 3:7-8). The contributors to the *International Theological Commentary* are persons who prize the writings of these biblical authors as a word of life to our world today. They read the Hebrew Scriptures in the twin contexts of ancient Israel and our modern day.

The scholars selected as contributors underscore the international aspect of the series. Representing very different geographical, ideological, and ecclesiastical backgrounds, they come from over seventeen countries. Besides scholars from such traditional countries as England, Scotland, France, Italy, Switzerland, Canada, New Zealand, Australia, South Africa, and the United States, contributors from the following places are included: Israel, Indonesia, India, Thailand, Singapore, Taiwan, and countries of Eastern Europe. Such diversity makes for richness of thought. Christian scholars living in Buddhist, Muslim, or Socialist lands may be able to offer the World Church insights into the biblical message — insights to which the scholarship of the West could be blind.

The proclamation of the biblical message is the focal concern of the *International Theological Commentary*. Generally speaking, the authors of these commentaries value the historical-critical studies of past scholars, but they are convinced that these studies by themselves are not enough. The Bible is more than an object of critical study; it is the revelation of God. In the written Word, God has disclosed himself and his will to humankind. Our authors see themselves as servants of the Word which, when rightly received, brings *shalom* to both the individual and the community.

Many people expect all Romanians to belong to the Orthodox Church. In the west of Romania, however, in the area that used to be known as Transylvania, there are quite large Reformed, Lutheran, and Roman Catholic communities. Professor Széles teaches Old Testament at the United Protestant Theological Seminary in the city of Cluj-Napoca. She is an example, par excellence, of the "international" element in this series. Her witness to the faith from within a Socialist society helps to redeem any parochial interpretations of Scripture others may quite unwittingly hold.

Neither Habakkuk nor Zephaniah is very well known or understood by our generation. These Old Testament prophets were contemporary with Jeremiah; that is, they interpreted the events that led up to the destruction of Jerusalem by Nebuchadnezzar, the Babylonian "king of kings and lord of lords," in 597 and 587 B.C.

What is unique about Professor Széles's study is that for the first time we have an "existential" interpretation of the mystery of God's apparent absence or weakness when his own people meet with intolerable suffering from the might of a cruel totalitarian regime.

Habakkuk makes a series of almost insolent complaints against God. In earlier days God had promised to give the land of Canaan to his people, Israel; to uphold his Covenant made with them at Sinai; to be "Father for ever" to David and his descendants. It now appeared that God had broken all his promises or was incapable of fulfilling them. After deep soul-searching, Habakkuk, from an inner "vision," declares that God's answer to his complaints is "decreed" and is now "hastening to its goal." God does not lie. Rather he makes use of evil men to his own glory and to further his purposes of redemption. But "the righteous shall live by his faith," and that faith will be seen as a transformation of a human being's whole personality.

Zephaniah notes the advance of the king of Babylon, who declares of himself, "I am, and there is none else." The prophet compares this statement with God's self-revelation to Moses as I AM. But an equally great arrogance shows itself in Jerusalem's own leaders. For they were wholly oblivious both to the cry of the poor and to their own greed and rapacity. In violating the Law of God they were in fact breaking the Covenant of old. Zephaniah announces God's judgment upon his own people and God's judgment upon all nations, for all mankind are sinners. But he also declares universal salvation once God reveals his unshakable loyalty to his chosen people; he will save them "for his own name's sake."

Most of the authors referred to by name in the text of her two commentaries have written in either German or Hungarian. Her references can be traced quite easily by those with access to a theological library (see the Bibliography). If the reference is to a work in English, then that volume is cited precisely. Some of her biblical quotations do not correspond with the English of the RSV. This is because they are direct translations from her Hungarian Bible.

GEORGE A. F. KNIGHT
FREDRICK CARLSON HOLMGREN

WATCHTOWER THEOLOGY

A Commentary on the Book of
Habakkuk

I will take my stand on my watchtower,
and look forth to see what he will say to me,
and what I will answer concerning my complaint.
—Habakkuk 2:1

CONTENTS

INTRODUCTION

HABAKKUK'S PERIOD AND PERSON

It was at a critical period in Israel's history that Habakkuk's prophecy sounded forth. It was the year 612 B.C., when the sun of Assyria's glory finally set; for after just a short time there began the Neo-Babylonian empire's successful but short-lived orbit. This was in the last decade of the 7th century B.C. and in the first years of the 6th century. It brought destruction and complete annihilation upon Israel. The year 609 forms one boundary that we can be sure of in relationship to the period of the prophet's service. That was the year when King Josiah lost the battle at Megiddo and so was the year of his death. The other is the year 597, when the first deportation of Jerusalem's citizens to Babylon took place. This threw a shadow over the period that ended in 587 with the final fall of the city. Josiah's reform of the cult in 622 had fallen into oblivion. The pure worship of Yahweh had been outwardly combined once again with pagan elements. Public morality had also crumbled; the prophet sees this happening (Hab. 1:2-4), and his contemporary, Jeremiah, declares this to be so too (Jer. 5:26-29; 7:1-15).

After Josiah's death, Pharaoh Neco II of Egypt initiated repressive activity, as is evident when, at Riblah, he "put in bonds" King Jehoahaz, the lawful successor to the throne (2 Kgs. 23:31-33), and placed Eliakim on the throne instead. The latter turned out for a while to be a subservient vassal. The tribute he laid upon the nation proved to be a heavy burden on the economic life of the country, reduced as it now was in size. In any case Eliakim was a useless ruler. He was extravagant with money, politically irresponsible, and repressive (Jer. 22:13-19; 26:20-23; 36), so as merely to deepen the moral and religious crisis. Nebuchadnezzar's victory at Carchemish, in 605, put the seal finally upon Assyria's fate while destroying the power of Egypt's armies, whom the fleeing Assyrians had sought to aid at Haran. This disruption of the balance of power between the world powers affected Judah too (Jer. 36:9); and because of the Babylonian victory Jehoiakim had to become a vassal of the Babylonians. In the following years Babylon and Egypt spent their time quarreling. Once when Nebuchadnezzar won an indecisive battle with Neco II Eliakim saw that the moment had arrived to throw off the feudal yoke and to give up paying tribute. But meanwhile the Babylonians gained new strength and retaliated. In 597 their army stormed and took Jerusalem. They deported Jehoiakin, along with his court, the government officials, and the treasures of the capital, to Babylon (2 Kgs. 24:8-16).

Although the heading of Habakkuk's prophecy (1:1) does not give a precise time, we can conclude from the coherent argument of the book that it points to this moment in history. This religious, political, and socio-ethical crisis characterizes the prophet's first complaint (1:2-4); because of the state of affairs in Jehoiakim's rule, he predicted that the punishment would be "brought about" by the LORD (1:6). The name the "punishers" was applied to the Chaldeans, the Neo-Babylonian empire, and refers to their terrorizing army. Through this characterization as described by the prophet at 1:5-17, and from the announcement of the punishment decided upon (2:6-20; 3:13-14), we know it was that particular great power which, after the fall of Assyria (612, 605), stepped with its terrifying military might on to the stage of world history, snatching quickly at fast-fading glory.

Against this interpretation of the date, B. Duhm, in 1906, tendered the new hypothesis that Habakkuk deals with the end of the 4th century; he was followed by several German and Hungarian scholars. The basis of this view is that the word Chaldeans (*Kasdim* in Hebrew) that occurs in 1:6 is to be read as Kittim. That name derived from Kittion, a city on the island of Cyprus. The Greeks on Cyprus came to use it as the symbol of their culture. On the basis of this reading B. Duhm and his followers understood the whole prophecy as reflecting the campaigns of Alexander the Great, who, after the battle of the Issus (333), hastened toward Gaugamela (331) and became the victorious lord of the world.

But evidence against this late dating of the prophecy in the 4th century was discovered in 1947, when the text of Habakkuk was found among the Dead Sea Scrolls along with a commentary upon it (1QpHab), exhibiting the spelling of the word as *Kasdim*. This is despite the fact that the unknown commentator, who was strongly influenced by his waiting for the "last times," uses the term Kasdim to refer to his own period and to those who are violently hellenizing the Jewish community.

Today, then, biblical scholars place Habakkuk's prophetic period in the last decade of the 7th century and in the first decade of the 6th century, between 609 and 597 B.C.

We have defined the period of the prophet's ministry; we shall now seek to discover what we can about his person. The heading of the book is very succinct. Apart from his name and his calling it offers us no further facts. His father's name is missing, as is his place of origin; there is nothing to indicate the circumstances of his life. The meaning of his name, *Habaqquq*, or in the LXX *Ambakoum*, is doubtful and debatable. It seems to derive from the root *hbq*, "embrace, comprehend, enfold, clasp to the heart." So it might mean "embraced," a person who is folded to another's heart. Jerome translates by the Latin *amplexus*, Luther by the German *Herzer*. According to this etymology the prophet is he who feels for his people at the time of their trial, takes them in his arms, so to speak, and undertakes to share their fate. But it could also mean, as becomes clear from the prophecy itself, that by his complaints and his challenges he actually "fights with God," directly wrestles with him. Other scholars suggest that the name is Akkadian in origin, *hambaququ*, meaning fragrant, used of a basil-like flower, *ocimum canum*, which flourished throughout Babylonia and was used for healing wounds. Thus it might refer to a specific green vegetable, such as a gourd or a cucumber, which was eaten as a food.

In the apocryphal literature, the "Addition" to the book of Daniel, "Bel and the Dragon" (vv. 33-39), mentions a man named Habakkuk. The angel of God carried him off by the forelock, bore him through the air, and set him down with food for Daniel when the latter was in the lion's den.

There is another indication of Habakkuk's person in the word *nabi'*, "prophet." He was the LORD's spokesman then, called, trained, and commissioned to be his messenger. He had received his prophetic calling through the instrumentality of the liturgy in public worship, had grasped it as it applied to himself, as it was visually and audibly mediated to him. Thereupon he communicated it to the worshiping congregation (2:1-5). This leads to the conclusion that he was a "cultic prophet" at the Jerusalem temple. Rudolph casts doubt upon this characterization, though the most recent commentaries all accept this conclusion.

It is indisputable that Habakkuk received his call in Jerusalem and that his whole period of service was connected with the tem-

5

ple. It was there, even as he performed his office, that he accepted the revelation and passed it on to the worshiping community (2:1-5).

Habakkuk's individuality as a prophet reveals two features — he is a praying person and he is a seeing person. His prophecies are composed in the form of the prayers such as we see in the "psalms of complaint" used in public worship. They are a theophany perceived in a vision and grasped audibly. Elements of Jeremiah's "Confessions" (Jer. 11:18ff.; 12:1ff.; 15:10ff.; 17:12ff.; 18:19ff.; 20:7ff.) can be discerned in our prophet's complaint as well as the argumentative sound of the psalms of complaint. He contends and argues as later on Job does with God and with his friends. Such argumentative prayers occur throughout the Psalter and are the theme that is to be found in common with the agonizing of Job — how to understand the righteousness of God, and to do so in a life-and-death struggle. Habakkuk is the type of the true sufferer, *tsaddiq*. He is rooted in his environment and suffers from a double burden. On the one hand he must witness the collapse of his era (1:2-4); on the other he must recognize that he who is of "purer eyes than to behold evil" (1:13), the holy LORD, turns his eyes away from the evil and remains silent "when the wicked swallows up the man more righteous than he." Habakkuk, "the man who sees," receives "the report" of God (3:2, 16) as a shock to his manhood, experiencing it by both seeing it and hearing it at the same time.

Habakkuk the prophet is an educated man. His prayers (ch. 3) especially show how well acquainted he is with the historical traditions of his people (Exod. 15:1-21; Deut. 33:2; Josh. 3:16; 10:12-13; Judg. 5), but he also knows the creation myths of the Babylonians and the Canaanites, as well as their gods — Baal, Yam, Anat, Marduk, Tiamat, all of whom are implied in ch. 3.

Especially prominent is the prophet's understanding of moral issues as well as his deep humanity (1:3-4, 14-17). Outstanding too are his "five woes" that occur one after the other in 2:6-19. His defense of the purely human emerges wherever human dignity is hurt and from whatever angle. The stance he takes and the arguments he adduces touch upon the humanity not just of Israel but of all mankind. The constantly recurring use of the term *mishpat* indicates that justice is meant for all mankind. Agonizing and wrestling in his prayers, the prophet in every case looks to God, the sovereign Lord of history, even as he observes humanity and empathizes with them. He is the God who revives his work "in the midst of the years" and "makes it known" (3:2).

It is just because he is the God who "in wrath remembers mercy" that Israel can have a future at all.

THE BOOK OF THE PROPHET HABAKKUK

Our prophet's book is quite unique among all the prophetic literature both in form and in content. It is noticeable that we do not find in it prophecies couched in the "messenger's speech" formulas. On the basis of his commissioning by Yahweh Habakkuk would have been expected to utter such to the covenant people, or to foreign peoples, as was customary in prophetic preaching. Instead they appear in the shape of a personal psalm of complaint, a prophetic oracle, or a hymn showing an amalgam of visual and audible elements in a dialogue that the prophet carries on with God.

Why his book was placed eighth among the "Book of the Twelve Prophets" is one of the great problems in the area of OT introduction.

We have looked at the questions that arise from defining the dating of the book. But the prophecy also presents us with problems about the relationship of its independent parts. Clearly we cannot speak of the literary unity of the three chapters, nor can we regard the whole as a mere collection of prophetic speeches. What is conspicuous, however, is not the unity of its form but of its contents, for that fuses together all the separate parts: Yahweh is the Lord of history who in a sovereign manner directs the fate of his people and brings to their conclusion his inscrutable plans. These in man's eyes remain a mystery and can be understood only in terms of faith.

The prophecy may be dissected into two independent parts. Chapters 1 – 2 may be regarded as a lament in the form of a psalm of complaint. In answer to it there comes the oracle which follows as a prophetic prediction. Complaint and oracle alternate with one another in the form of a personal dialogue.

The prophet's first complaint is contained in 1:2-4. It is an urgent cry for help expressed to Yahweh because of the moral crisis that Habakkuk has experienced among his people. This is followed by an oracle that announces (in 1:5-11) the judgment of a punishment of slavery upon the Judeans. Once again a complaint follows in vv. 12-17, containing elements of repeated accusations expressed with the vigorous emphasis of a prophet who is truly human. Upon this there follows that reassuring, definitive answer of 2:1-5, which the prophet hears as he stands on his watchtower. It is that Yahweh is aware of the judgment that reaches into the future, that the "righteous" shall live by his faith. He will bring this about despite all the successes of the "puffed up" enemy. The second complaint, in 2:6-20, is then closed with a "woe song," characteristic of the dirge in the shape in which it occurs in the *mashal* (parable) literature (e.g., Ps. 78:2), and so stands as a witness to his prophetic "listening."

Any judgment on the unity of the first two chapters would, it seems, be problematical. Recent commentaries suggest many solutions: some that these chapters were meant to be employed in the temple worship; others emphasize the dialogue element in them; while others point out that the passage 2:3-4 is the essence of what is then expanded in 2:5-20 to make the prophet's central message plain to all, particularly to reveal Yahweh's sovereign will to the cultic community of Israel.

Chapter 3 is the second independent section of the prophecy, and its literary unity reveals itself as a separate art form. It is a theophany expressed in the form of a prayer. This piece has its own heading (3:1) and closes with its own separate musical direction for use in public worship (3:19b). This prayer gives a description of a festal revelation of the LORD who comes and dispenses justice to his people through victory over their enemies. In both seeing and hearing, the prophet's whole personality experiences the appearance of the LORD in a shattering manner (3:2, 16).

The two independent sections of the prophecy are held together organically. The point of connection between the two separate parts is 2:20. In that verse the prophet summons the whole created world to keep silence before the LORD upon his throne in the temple, for he is coming to conquer his enemies by exercising his royal prerogative. This connection is evidenced by the introduction to the prophet's first complaint: "O LORD, how long shall I cry" (1:2), for it shows a forward look to the theophany that is to take place.

The second individual, collective complaint, whose motif refers to the very being of God (v. 12), is consonant with the features of God's "saving history" that we read about in 3:2ff. The vision through which the LORD presents his decisive answer with respect to the future (2:1-4, 5-20) would not be comprehensible without ch. 3. The motif of creation, of Yahweh in his own person as the Creator, is emphasized in the unity of the two sections (1:14; 3:8, 11-12).

In the manner characteristic of the prophetic literature, ch. 3

shows to what an extent Habakkuk too has absorbed the traditions of his people; yet at the same time we see how well acquainted he is with the mythological concepts of his environment. He refers to significant events in salvation history (Exod. 15:1-21; Deut. 33:2; Josh. 3:16; 10:12-13; Judg. 5), even employing the concise, ballad style of the period. The prophet identifies himself so profoundly with these events that they appall his whole being (3:2, 16) and actually lead to the disintegration of his personality. Yet as the final outcome of this shattering experience there emerges an overflowing joy (3:18). Indeed, his diction accommodates itself here; it expresses his ecstatic experience in apocalyptic-mythic language.

This unity is witnessed to indirectly in the Habakkuk Scroll and Commentary (1QpHab), one of the Dead Sea Scrolls found at *'Ain Feshkha,* though it contains only chs. 1 and 2. The point is that the unknown commentator belonging to the Qumran sect, who kept before his eyes the events of his own, first-century B.C. historical circumstances when he interpreted these chapters, started from the theological concepts of his sect, and so was not able to associate the universal eschatological views in ch. 3 with his own narrow viewpoint. Since the commentator held to the rigid dualism of the Persians, he could conceive of Yahweh's salvation as applying only to those who were specifically followers of the Teacher of Righteousness. On the other hand the psalm in ch. 3 refers to Yahweh's mercy, to his grace that is to appear "in the midst of the years." So the Qumran scribe left out this chapter from his copy so as not to have to comment on it.

The oracles included in Habakkuk's book, just as is the case with the rest of the prophetic writings, came into being at various times. These prophecies of various genres have been systematically edited by a redactor in the postexilic period. Without any doubt the stamp of the theological views of the prophet himself refers to the events of his time, and that stamp is here in his book. We would suggest that in his book Habakkuk, as a cult prophet, gives us a faithful picture of his service as a prophet, mediating as he does his LORD's declarations. Rudolph's view is that the following verses originate from a later period: 2:6a, 8b, 13a; 14:18-20; 3:2b, 4b, 7a, 8a, 17-19.

THE THEOLOGY OF HABAKKUK

Habakkuk's prophetic material appears in its own individualistic form, quite as if we were hearing the sound of his voice, unique among prophetic preaching. Yet the accustomed formulations of prophetic literature, "Thus says the LORD," or, "Hear the word of the LORD," are missing with him, though his witness fits into the line of the prophets and enriches their many-colored content.

Essentially each prophecy is a dialogue in which the prophet as spokesman mediates between the covenanting God and his people. God's presence becomes evident to the people of the prophet's period through this prophetic service as he preaches both God's judgment and his mercy. In this way Yahweh's royal prerogative intervenes and his will is effected. This remarkable and peculiar character is apparent in Habakkuk's prophecies, but it is also the penetrating stamp of the whole OT proclamation. C. Westermann would suggest that this dialogue between God and his people is actually *the* structural feature peculiar to the whole OT (see, e.g., *Elements of Old Testament Theology*, tr. D. W. Stott [Atlanta: John Knox Press, 1982]).

Not only the prophetic material but also Israel's Wisdom literature and even the historical writings make it clear that humanity is evil by nature and very fragile; in every situation mankind is dependent upon their saving God. Whenever they are in straits and cry out, Yahweh, the Savior, answers them with his grace. This deed of his, moreover, always solicits from human beings thanksgiving and praise. Complaint and exaltation from such persons are a revelation that witnesses to the way in which God embraces them in his liberating deeds. A complaint in time of distress, or when experiencing the approach of death, rouses God as a cry for help. An expression of praise at the moment of liberation rises up from the human heart as a sign of life. It expresses gratitude for grace experienced. Liberation is a proof of Yahweh's power and belongs to his nature just as its opposite belongs to the frailty of man's humanity that is made evident in his "complaint and exaltation."

In Habakkuk's prophecy such dialogue is a concrete theme. It represents the theological content of the whole prophecy. This theme is the existential question of Habakkuk's prophetic understanding of history — the testing of the devout, the *tsaddiq*, who, with respect to his faith, his '*emunah*, is victorious in his steadfastness against temptation. Where does the testing come from? How does the crisis end up? These are the prophecy's basic questions; within their compass the content of his theology is securely positioned.

The first motif leading to this crisis of faith is to be found in the prophet's first complaint (1:2-4); he complains of the "righteous" person's futile, useless knocking on the doors of the *Deus absconditus* who does not listen. Just how much must one rouse God up in a time of distress? Why must one regard helplessly the course of events in the life of the community when Yahweh could put a stop to it but does not? The LORD's inexplicable silence and passivity plunges the prophet into a state of crisis. In his complaint he exposes the social and moral/ethical situation as indicative of total corruption. Man's dignity has been manifoldly injured and rendered impotent in all aspects of community life. The prophet's profound humanity reveals itself before our eyes in his sympathetic emphasis upon moral issues. Habakkuk's re-action to experiences arising directly from his times goes in two directions. The first is a lively objection to the ill-treatment people have to go through from their fellow human beings — when they experience wrongs done to them and have to suffer from human violence (1:3). The second is a violent rejection of the arbitrary power of the administrators of the law and of the experience of suffering from the perversion of justice. Here the word *mishpat* covers the whole area of human rights; it arises from *yir' at Yahweh*, the "fear of the LORD."

The second motif that plunged the prophet into crisis is the manner of Yahweh's working, in that he punishes the "wicked." It is about this punishment that he complains. The prophet's agonizing question is this — can a tyrant be overcome through a still more evil despot? How can the God of law and of right-eousness choose such an instrument for the administration of justice? Between the prophet's complaint and the LORD's answer there exists an unbridgeable chasm, resulting in an ever-deep-ening and ever-maddening crisis. Suffering from these torments, and at the same time in rebellion against them, the prophet re-veals the impatient attitude of the *tsaddiq*. For him the question is not whether God can intervene in events, but whether such ways of behavior should be so incomprehensible that God should need to incorporate himself in world events in order to bring his miraculous acts to a conclusion. Habakkuk's moral concern is evident here. Not only does he introduce Yahweh in his deposition from the point of view of ethics (1:13), he also gives an ethical motivation to his complaint (1:13-15).

The prophet as he bears witness regards righteous character in the sphere of human relationships as the measure of history. This is expressed through prophetic preaching and is the basic reality arising from the saving history of Israel. It is only a right-eous character that can prove the truth of God's divinity, man's

11

humanity, and, in connection with the two, the meaning of life. There is no greater distress than when power ordained for the service of justice makes injustice legal. In Habakkuk's state of anguish is contained the whole band of prophets as suffering seekers for a new heaven and a new earth.

From out of this crisis, about which the LORD is incomprehensibly silent, there arises a strange course of action — there is no way out! It is God alone who can provide the solution. Habakkuk prepares himself to receive the answer. Instead of complaining and disputing he becomes quiet, and on his watchtower he awaits the LORD's reply. Yahweh's answer (2:2-5) is an announcement, a prophecy of redemption which in its content is more than, and in quality different from, the answer given to the questions put through the prophet. God gives no reasons for his silence, nor does he explain his compulsion to act in this strange manner; rather, as the Lord of world history, he proclaims his will in a sovereign manner. This is what the prophet on his watchtower must convey before all else to the worshiping community, that the LORD has spoken, breaking his long silence. Thereafter he is to write out the "vision" that is still to come. It will come to pass in God's own specified time *(mo'ed)*. This announcement places the future in a double light. "Behold, the puffed up — he will no longer have life, but the righteous shall live by his faith."

According to Habakkuk's witness the solution of the crisis can come about through faith alone. The prophet picks out from the OT concept of faith a concentration on trustful endurance and steadfastness. In the prophet's theology *'emunah* means, instead of querulousness and argumentation, obedient bowing before the LORD. The LORD's actions are incomprehensible to the human mind, yet at the same time they are accompanied by confidence in him and resolute perseverance with him. In the prophet's situation, to believe means "to be made strong in the LORD," to hold on, to find security in time of trial; and besides to possess faithful perseverance even when his wondrous deeds are incomprehensible. This is the faith "that is the assurance of things hoped for, the conviction of things not seen" (Heb. 11:1). This manner of behavior is the "real" way of life whose *modus vivendi* opens up the future. Habakkuk's confession speaks of the purpose of life. History and life, faith and life: faith triumphant over fate — this is the essence of the OT conception of life.

Habakkuk's prophecy closes with a prayer. It is a kind of psalm from the cult extolling the mighty LORD who will come to execute his judgment. The prophet, who had stood on his watchtower and had waited, watching in agitation for an answer to his complaint, now hears with dismay the report of the judgment and sees its execution. When it happens, it will shake all humanity (3:2, 16); it will bring forth a prayer on his lips, impel him to deep gratitude, while, looking to the future with trust, he will be filled with the joy of salvation.

Habakkuk's prophecy portrays the LORD's face with forceful features — with features that his people recognized in his saving acts throughout the history of salvation. This picture is one with the witness that Israel's prophets had made plain. Yahweh is the only living and holy LORD (2:18; 1:12; cf. Isa. 6:3; Ezek. 20:12; Isa. 41:14; 43:3; 48:17; 1 Kgs. 20:36-39; Hos. 11:9). He summons nations and stations them in positions of service (Hab. 1:6; 5:5; Jer. 27:7; 29:28; 51:20; Isa. 10:5; 7:18-20). He is the Creator of the world (Hab. 1:14; 3:10-11; Isa. 45:7; 65:17; 42:5; 43:7; Jer. 27:5; 31:22; Ezek. 28:13, 15; Mal. 2:10). At the same time he is in covenant with his people (Hab. 3:13; Amos 3:2; Hos. 11:1-4; Isa. 43:1-7; Jer. 2:1, 12; 7:1, 7).

Habakkuk's God, as the unquestionably powerful, sovereign LORD, is he who has the power to hide himself in silence, in impotence, in extraordinary events beyond human understanding, yet who, when he decides to, can step forth and reveal himself. In the end the LORD does reveal his Being and his mode of existence, giving his complaining and disputatious prophet a comforting answer as he stands on his watch. There is but one possibility for understanding and grasping the LORD's "report," and that is through 'emunah, through the prophet's loyal witness to his deep "faith." This faith is to be not only the means of carrying one through the burdensome days but also the pledge that one really possesses life. It shows that the people are indeed called by God when their lifestyle stands in firm continuity with such a calling.

The prophet surveys this lifestyle in an expressive picture. It describes a deer that leaps insouciantly and confidently over steep cliffs and deep chasms. The person of "faith" is set free of his burdens, saved from his afflictions. He walks in confidence, because his life has been established upon a new foundation. He goes upon such "heights" that no depths can make him dizzy (3:18-19).

"A theology on a watchtower, a theology upon the bastion" (2:1) could be said to be Habakkuk's prophetic word to the *tsaddiq*, who has been called to belong in the Covenant. He is to bear witness out of temptation and crisis to the victory that comes through 'emunah.

13

COMMENTARY

THE HEADING (1:1)

Habakkuk's own particular tone and prophetic content place their stamp even upon the book's heading. Alongside mention of the prophet's name, which is of uncertain meaning, we find a reference to his prophetic character only in the word *massa'*, "oracle" in the RSV, though a more exact description of him is that of *nabi'*, "prophet." As such he "sees," *hazah*, in a vision what the LORD "says to me" (2:1). We have no nearer facts to go upon about his period or his person, or about the circumstances of his life. See the Introduction to learn about the book's structure.

The term *massa'* shows the book's prophetic character. It stems from the verb *nasa'*, meaning lift up, carry. In a legal sense it is used of the administration of justice by a leader or a by a judge or by the authorities (*nasi'*; cf. Exod. 22:17); hence it has the sense "lift up the voice," "proclaim," "communicate," "reveal," "burden one with a judgment" (Jer. 23:3-40; Lam. 2:14). Yet it brings together all that judgmental prophecy which Yahweh's prophet conveys to Israel or to the pagan nations as his chosen and commissioned agent. Understood in this way, then, *massa'* is a technical term for interpreting to the prophet the LORD's judgment (cf. Isa. 13:14; 15:1; Nah. 1:1; Zech. 9:1; 12:1; Mal. 1:1).

So in Yahweh's decree as Judge and in his pronouncement of judgment Habakkuk "sees" *(hazah)*, that is, he reviews the judgment in a prophetic vision. The verb *hazah* is used expressly for a prophetic vision. In it God sets forth the object of his concern before his prophet. This observation applies to the whole prophecy—to chs. 1–2 but especially to the theophany in ch. 3. The prophet Habakkuk is thus a "seer." With peculiar intensity he "experiences" Yahweh's "report" both audibly and visually. It was undoubtedly in the period after the Exile, when the prophecies were collected and edited, that this descriptive term was applied to explain the nature of the prophecy.

The prophet awaited the report in the holy place, the "watch"

15

or the "tower" (2:1). It had to be written on "tablets" so that everyone could read it easily; it indicates that Habakkuk was in Jerusalem, serving at the temple as a "cultic prophet" and conveying the will of God to the worshiping community.

COMPLAINT AND ORACLE (1:2– 2:20)

The first independent part of Habakkuk's prophecy comprises chs. 1 and 2. It contains a dialogue conducted between God and his prophet. In the Introduction we noted various opinions on this issue. Since we have reviewed this question and that of the prophet's person and service as these can be discovered from his book, we can see that the dialogue in chs. 1 and 2 is conceived in the form of a prophetic liturgy. This the prophet carries on with God in the execution of his (temple?) service. The two ongoing dialogues, after Yahweh's final answer is imparted (2:1-5), are closed in an appendix found in 2:6-20 by an oracle indicating the certainty of having been heard. This prepares for the theophany in ch. 3 and for Yahweh's announcement of ultimate victory.

Elements of psalms of complaint and motifs of prophetic oracles combine in a characteristic manner. This is clearly a deliberate work of editing in which the prophet's complaint and the LORD's answer follow each other with regularity. The dialogue begins with the setting forth of an urgent, impatient complaint (1:2-4), followed by an extraordinary reply (1:5-11). This develops into an appeal (1:12-17), after which there follows the LORD's definitive reply (2:1-5). Then comes the oracle (2:6-20) that conveys judgment upon the "arrogant," the punishment for their deeds.

The text of chs. 1– 2 may be divided as follows:
1. Complaints of oppression and violence, 1:2-4
2. Oracle on the judgment delivered about the nature of power, 1:5-11
3. Appeal, 1:12-17
4. Yahweh's final answer, 2:1-5
5. Dirge over the doomed tyrant, 2:6-20

Complaints of Oppression and Violence (1:2-4)

In the form of a psalm of complaint by an individual this pericope is a prayer that speaks out about suffering. Right at the beginning of his prophecy Habakkuk's very personal, striking features appear, and these leave traces upon the whole of his preaching — he is the person who wrestles in prayer. This accent of his calls to mind his contemporary, Jeremiah, and his "confessions" (Jer. 11:18-23; 12:1-3; 5-6; 15:10-12, 21; 17:12-18; 18:18-23; 20:7-18), as well as Job's challenges of God and of his friends. In the psalmist's literature we have the recurring motif of the "righteous" *(tsaddiq)* wrestling in a bitter tone, taking God to task as he seeks to understand the justice of Yahweh.

The structure of this pericope is: the buildup, the question, the description of the situation, and the final drawing of the conclusion.

The questioning sentences put in the manner of the psalms of complaint lead to the particular cries: ʿ*ad* ʿ*anah,* "How long?", and *lammah,* "Why?" These little words refer on the one hand to the present period of unbearable corruption, and on the other hand to justification before God. The root *shw*ʿ in its intensive form here means a cry for help, in fact, just "Help!" It is a seeking urgently for rescue from deadly danger. The prophet does not doubt God's might, as if he were unable to rescue; what agitates him is that he has received no answer to the cry he has raised so often. How long will Yahweh remain silent, when the patience of him who prays is gradually being exhausted under the load he carries? *Z*ʿ*q* means to shout, to scream, to roar. One may concretize the complaint in a few words: "the law is being trampled upon." *Hamas* is deliberate, planned oppression, exploitation, terrorizing, holding the law in contempt. The prophet is urging Yahweh to give an ear in his silence, to intervene and to arbitrate. *Ysh*ʿ means help, rescue from an existential danger, save, preserve a human life. The verbal root envisages the greatness of the danger: it is human life that is at stake.

The second question, *lammah,* "Why?", is focused rather on the prophet's spiritual crisis. Why does God allow evil men to indulge in such orgies? Why does God let Habakkuk see all this? The prophet agonizes over the fact that he sees with his own eyes the moral collapse of his time. The prophet not only observes this critical situation — he knows he must examine it as God displays it before him. There it is in reality, a situation immune from every human subjectivity. The verbs *rʾh* and *nbt* in its Hiphil (causative) form show that it is Yahweh, so to speak, who displays the actual situation before his prophet and lays it upon his moral sensitivity.

In this extreme situation Habakkuk protests against the contemporary trampling down of law and seeks for a cure in this period of misery. His complaint reveals in what way public life has broken down; it speaks of how all claims to human cooper-

17

ation have disappeared. Humanity has been impaired in its human dignity; one can no longer live a life worthy of man the creature of God. The prophet is interceding on behalf of humanity; in fact, his own humanity asserts itself in his first vigorous complaint. In it his characteristic ideas put their stamp on the injustice being done to Israel's legal existence. The ideas we find here are those that always arise in the course of the prophet's preaching with regard to questions of a social-ethical nature.

The *hamas* complained of refers to violent deeds as mirrored in the abuse of power that results in oppression and extortion. The issue here is the arbitrary and deliberate rejection of human rights — in a word, tyranny (cf. Gen. 34:13-15; 49:5; Amos 3:10; Prov. 4:17; the Priestly writer's word in Gen. 6:11, 13, "violence"). It is this concept that condenses and subsumes and ties together in convincing fashion the host of human sins, because of which God destroys the earth in the Flood. A nearly equivalent variation in this complaint occurs as the word *shod*. It means to wipe out or annihilate, and it refers to that which results from vigorous or violent repression (cf. Isa. 16:4; Hos. 7:13; Hab. 2:17; Job 5:21). The word *'awen* expresses human wickedness in the form of deceit, misrepresentation, deliberate misleading of someone so as to do him harm or cause him to suffer (Isa. 10:1; 59:4; Num. 23:21; Job 5:6). *'Amal* means weariness, exhaustion, enervation, a loss of vitality, collapse, caused not by any physical tiredness but by the hostile behavior of one's fellows that produces spiritual torture (cf. Ps. 73:16; Isa. 10:1; Hab. 1:13). All this the prophet observes from close at hand, *lenegdi*, "right in front of me." In such a baleful situation of physical-spiritual suffering, community life becomes impossible; instead it encourages lawsuits *(rib)* and wrangling *(madon)*. People devour each other, denounce one another to the authorities; everyone blames the other and in this way seeks to avert responsibility from himself. This description of moral corruption views it as a crisis on the horizontal plane, but the presentation on the vertical plane appears through an outlining of the ultimate outcome, which the prophet summons his fellows to regard as the real cause of the collapse.

An adverbial conjunction introduces v. 4: *'al-ken*, "therefore"; for this reason God's gracious teaching (i.e., the Torah), which he has offered to human beings for both their horizontal and their vertical relationships, has become "paralyzed," "frozen" *(pwg)*; it is no longer effective, because it is not allowed to be so.

The Torah, the document of the Covenant, Yahweh's incomparable gift granted only to the chosen people "for your good"

18

(Deut. 10:13), set forth the prescriptions for behavior toward both God and one's neighbors. And now, according to the prophet's judgment, it had become "paralyzed," rendered impotent, with no force to it. "When there is no heavenly vision, the people become unmanageable; but he who keeps the Law, oh, how truly blessed is he" (Prov. 29:18). This prophetic criticism expresses first a judgment against the charismatic leaders who "embezzle" the "Law" committed to their care. We can think of the period of Jehoiakim and the abuses then, of the moral and social crisis, of the seesaw political move from Egypt to Babylonia with the tyranny in the internal political situation that resulted. The prophet refers explicitly to the distortion of life under the law, to the absolutist administration of the law by the authorities. An unknown commentator on the Qumran Habakkuk (Dead Sea) Scroll (1QpHab) recognizes this internal political collapse. It was natural, from the relatively narrow theological stance of his time, to apply this to the enemies of the Teacher of Righteousness, so that the inner decay happened because of them. As a result of the false handling of the "Law," its being silenced, or as a result of the arbitrary interpretation of it, true justice *(mishpat)* by and large did not come to light *(yatsa')*. The "wicked" *(rasha')* had entrapped *(ktr)* their victim, the "righteous" *(tsaddiq)*, as in a spider's web. The performance of justice, the administration of the law *(mishpat)* had become warped and dislocated *(me'uqqal)*, and now showed itself in a distorted form. The verb *'aqal* that occurs here means make crooked, reverse something upon itself, distort. The Pual intensive participle denotes the complete distortion, the hopelessness of the prevailing situation under the law.

The prophet never names those who have brought about this situation. The *rasha'* remains anonymous. It is difficult to find one's way through the many identifications that have been made. It cannot refer to the Assyrians, because by Habakkuk's time they had disappeared from the stage of history (612, 605 B.C.). Babylonia too cannot enter into the reckoning, since according to Yahweh's ordinance they had to fulfill the role of "punisher" (1:6). One could think of Egypt in an indirect manner. When Josiah withstood them after the battle of Megiddo (609), they sought to punish him by dashing the hopes of the legitimate successor to the throne. The Egyptian pharaoh set his vassal Jehoiakim on it, while stripping him of his income as a vassal and crushing Judah. Because of this an enemy within hides behind the term "the wicked" — the royal court, top men beholden to Egyptian influence, priests who had lost their positions, courtiers who, in their own interests, for their own well-being and positions of power, did not allow the precepts of the Law to maintain their force.

It is in this situation that the prophet appeals to Yahweh, the God of the Covenant, and awaits from him the legal remedy, since he is the one and only source and guardian of the right (Deut. 1:17). The cause of this prayerful prophet's spiritual crisis was that he had already, again and again, cried for help, and his request had received no hearing. On the contrary, he could only review in actuality the trampling under foot of the "right" in every respect, and he had to live through the total collapse of the moral life of his time. The crisis even deepened when it became obvious to him that God, who was the God of righteousness and of the "right," had turned his eyes away from these orgies of wickedness. Only later, while standing — tensely gazing — on his watchtower (2:1-5), could he come to recognize that God, the living LORD, the God of life, *can* keep silence! All idols are dumb; only he who truly lives is capable of being silent!

Oracle on the Judgment Delivered about the Nature of Power (1:5-11)

God answers the prophet's complaint in the form of an oracle that foretells what is to come. It answers exactly what the complaint is about, in language characteristic of the psalm style. After the complaint follows a response that gives evidence that the complaint has been heard. Here the oracle, the prophetic foretelling, gives the reason for the silence. Yahweh does in fact reply — he does so in historical events; it is in the setting of world history that he portrays his answer. This answer means an astonishing violation of the form of the cultic tradition. Normally a complaint is presented to God through the mediation of a priest or a cultic prophet, with the result that his prayer puts an end to the sorrowful situation from within which the complaint was conceived. But here the crisis about which the prophet had complained and for which he sought punishment upon a repressive tyranny does not come to an end. Instead a still more cruel "evil" ruler steps into the foreground at the command of Yahweh (1:6). In powerful lunacy (1:15-17) he will execute a still more frightful outrage upon ordinary people. God speaks directly to his prophet, initiating him into his secrets, into his plans that are to be executed in the future (cf. Amos 3:7). This fact makes Habbakuk's designation as a "prophet" ever more real and defines it more exactly, despite the fact that we possess no further information about him. This address is uttered not just to the prophet personally, but through him to the worshiping community as well. Habakkuk's role as an intermediary is evident here. It is in the holy place that he performs his service as a charismatic — instructing the congregation both from his hearing and from his seeing what God says to him.

The pericope is built up as follows: introduction (v. 5); the characterization of God as punitive (vv. 6-10); summary and completion (v. 11).

Yahweh, whom the prophet has addressed as the God of the Covenant, is also Lord of the created world, the God of history; he directs attention to the events of world history. It is not a question of the LORD wanting to turn his prophet's attention away from those events which are both attractive and bewitching; rather, all along he has forced him to recognize through the manifestation of his power that he has no reason whatsoever to complain and to cry impatiently for succour. Alongside his agonizing cries of "How long?" and "Why?" he is to behold the sovereign Lord, whose work proceeds on the level of world events according to *his* might and unsearchable wisdom. The prophet will only too soon be eyewitness of this level of fearful events on a worldwide scope. Yahweh does not answer the prophet's piercing questions that cause agony to both body and soul and that result in a crisis, in that human sight is too narrow and moves only on the horizontal plane. These rather bear witness to the "royal prerogative." God has the power to act in this way and so by this means provide the answer.

With its three demands the introduction in v. 5 deals with the theme of the answer: "Look" *(re'u)*, "Consider" *(habbitu)*, "Wonder and be astonished." It is a mental attitude that is spoken of here, a preparing of one's mind to be in a state of readiness. The chosen people are to "look out" beyond their own situation and take notice of the pagan peoples *(goyim)*, and see what God is going to bring to pass there! The verb *tamah* means be astonished, fear, find the words sticking in one's throat, tighten up, grow dumb, become breathless with amazement. The Hithpael points to a collective sense of consternation, to the community's corporate bewilderment at seeing an extraordinary event. The tension is heightened with the words: "You would not believe it if told." Everything that is about to happen outstrips all human imagination. These are the wondrous works of Yahweh that the Psalms extol as his "mighty doings" (Ps. 30:5; 100:4; 106:1; 118:1, 29; 136:1; 147:7).

In vv. 6-10 in plain language we read the announcement of
Yahweh's extraordinary deeds: "For lo, I am rousing the Chaldeans." It is I, Yahweh says, who calls for them and sets them at
my service. The Hiphil participle *meqim*, from the root *qwm*, sol-
emnly indicates that Yahweh is he who endlessly "rouses up,"
summons, entrusts, and positions instruments for his service all
throughout history, and through them accomplishes his own work,
including his disciplinary and judicial activities. This is the same
idea as the First Isaiah produced a century before Habakkuk's
day, with reference to Assyria, "The rod of my anger; the staff
of my fury; a hired razor" (Isa. 10:5; 7:20). More than this the
prophet refers to God's acts in salvation history. In the time of
the Judges he had chastised his people for turning to idols, yet
had raised up his people's judges to bring deliverance. Brought
out of insignificance, from anonymity, they were to perform extraordinary deeds on the basis of their charismatic commission,
and to free their people from distress.

Bimekem, "in your days," means the nearness of events, their
unfolding to happen in the present. This is Yahweh's own "method
of working." The whole prophecy is dependent upon its central
question, as to why God uses *this* means of answering about the
accomplishment of his plan. Why should he put his judgment in
motion just through that "Great Power," the Chaldeans? It is at
this point that the prophet is scandalized and because of that
contends with God. This people is not tractible in the hands of
the holy LORD; it obeys its own natural being, which is quite
foreign to the holy and pure Being of Yahweh. It strives only to
accomplish its own mission.

The characterization of this Great Power that is being used for
punishment happens in the mirror of its acts. God informs the
prophet about what this people is going to do, what its motives
are, and what will be the result of its action. In this summary
the inner motives of the outward acts are brought to light along
with the effects of these acts. "Motive" and "fruit" are the beginning and end of every action.

In v. 6 the word *mar*, bitter, poisonous, savage, merciless, describes an action in general and as seen externally. *Nimhar* means
hasty, rushing, tempestuous. Because of its speed, staggering occurs. As part of this conception we see the advance of a mob,
staggering because of their speed. These are all external signs
rousing terror in people. Everywhere and in all directions they
march through the land to make it their own. In their feverish
desire to keep on ransacking and violently confiscating the peo-

ple's worldly goods (this is shown in an expressive wordplay, *lo'-lo*, "not their own") is depicted their struggles to conquer. The prophet's humanity resounds here when his neighbor's material possessions need protection.

Verse 7 gives us a description of the core of the issue and points to the inner nerve of events. *'Ayom* means terrible, fearful; *nora'* means ghastly, alienating; it reveals the fear in the inner heart caused by events. The Chaldeans are completely "autonomous," not recognizing law of any kind except what the exercise of their own mood dictates. In other words, nothing keeps them in check, in either a legal or a moral sense. They are a law unto themselves, a law that knows no rules. They forsake every regulation; they flout every infringement, paying no attention to them whatsoever.

This inner disposition explains their outward behavior: an unquenchable craving to seize possession and a passion for plunder. This is clearly shown in three images. *Namer* is a leopard; nimbly and stealthily it pounces on its prey, an idea expressed by *qll*. After fasting all day the evening wolf, *ze'eb 'ereb*, seeks passionately for its prey and refuses to give up till he has found it. *Nesher* means eagle or vulture. From far off it can scent a dead animal and hurry to seize it. The result of such passionate and rapacious greed is seen in pitiless acts, the collecting together of masses of plunder and of crowds of prisoners of war. These cannot be numbered, for they are like the sand of the sea (v. 9).

They march on like a hurricane; they come with the deliberate purpose of violence, relentlessly pillaging beyond and outside all law, exercising *hamas*, violence, oppression, exploitation. From the angle of his humanity the prophet here too takes the side of the weak. Such fanatical behavior is pictured by one particular feature. They persist in their determination — an astonishing perseverance, *megammat penehem qadimah*, "the ambition of their faces is before them" (note that the RSV sees this line as "uncertain"). In other words, "Nothing, at any price, can divert them." So the wicked have their own logic and consistency! But the result of their rapine and plundering is immeasurable hurt.

Verses 10 and 11 also show insight into the inner man and his realm of feeling. The prophet portrays the laughable nature of a great power: the cynical despot, the sneering manner in which he laughingly seizes booty for himself. He contemptuously exerts his power upon kings and monarchs, as the object of his sneering and humiliating attention. This is a masterly portrayal of the totally self-confident, arrogant person, who sees himself upon a distinctive eminence, always supposing that for him everything is possible. Such is the prophetic conceptualizing of demonic power, when power and he who exercises it become divine. This situation cannot last without punishment. In v. 7 the prophet "summarizes" by declaring that he who regards his power as god worships his own might as a god and so "falls into sin." '*Asham* suggests trespass, debt, the weight of sin, in which the weight is the sin's own punishment. God calls to account, to the recognition of one's responsibility, for no sin can remain without its punishment. The end of the mighty is that he falls in his own successes! His very successes actually dig his grave into which he irretrievably rushes. Once again we meet with the tension of opposites: he who is the means of producing judgment partakes of judgment; the ruthless tyrant (according to 1:2-4) partakes of still greater "destruction and violence." One form of God's judgment is that the violent must be confronted with his own sin—he must taste what violence means.

Appeal (1:12-17)

The prophet repeats his complaint once again; it becomes an appeal with reference to the answer he has received. It is not to be regarded as an outspoken objection or reproach, in the sense of *tokahat,* the last word in 2:1, meaning reprimand, censure, claim. It is coupled with the motif of a hymn of praise (1:12), in which the prophet expresses his trust. Though the prophet several times exhibits impatient haste (1:2-4), he does not expect a corresponding answer, nor does he look for a satisfactory reply; rather, he employs an appeal. In the form of a hymn, his "Why?" appears in contrast with his conception of God's witness when Yahweh answers by announcement of the fierce and threatening service of the enemy. The prophet is sure that his complaint has met with a listening ear, and he takes note of the LORD's intervention and execution of judgment. The problem for the prophet is the *manner* in which God will execute his judgment, why he should stretch out his hand to use an instrument that is unworthy of his pure and holy Being. The style of the pericope is that of a personal psalm of complaint, a hymn, and a prophetic utterance about the contemporary historical situation. The prophet's moral concern and his deep humanity are also apparent here. So its structure is: hymn and complaint (vv. 12-13); Habakkuk's reflection on the historical situation (vv. 14-16); the prophet's bewildered concluding question (v. 17).

The interrogative particle *halo*', "Art thou not," begins vv. 12-14. The question shows an affinity with the previous complaint at 1:2-4, which began with the words "How long?" and "Why?" Only there he expressed impatience, uncertainty, while here he reveals his perplexity and ignorance. The LORD's behavior is a riddle to him, just because he knows who this God is, about whom he again bears witness in a passionate note. The pious Israelite elucidates the Being of Yahweh from the angle of the faith of the covenant people. This faith is born when the covenant people recognize the deeds of the LORD, both reflecting them and being nourished from them. Just because of this relationship, this picture constructed about God is not a static description but a sketch of a dynamic event.

One particular key concept is expressed in the word *miqqedem*, "from days of old that are past," that have been ever since the beginning, from time immemorial. In this word, then, the prophet expresses God's eternity of being — in fact, his timelessness. This is a close reference to him as the Creator God (v. 14; Gen. 1:26, 28) who from his creative power deals with the whole earth and is responsible for all its creatures (Ps. 24). This means that God who at creation stepped into history and through the channel of his acts bore witness about himself remains unchangeably and always the same (Exod. 3:14; Deut. 32:40). According to Israel's faith this ever-present yet transcendent God, the LORD who is always living *in* his deeds, is he who in a marvelous manner has borne his people throughout the course of history. Thus Yahweh's eternity is revealed as active Being, the living Reality revealed in his deeds. The prophet's witness therefore is to the living God. He alone, who truly lives, only he can work in this way.

The solution connected with this line of thought was that the prophet had accepted the fact that God calls to account and punishes people for deterioration of their social relationships. The Lord of history can choose his instrument of punishment from among the peoples so that even a cruel nation such as they can administer his justice, even though his choice may seem incomprehensible to us. If we take note of the historical circumstances of the prophet's time this portrayal fits exactly what we read about in the earlier pericope. After the destruction of Assyria in 605, Nebuchadnezzar's hosts, the Great Power, frequently turned up in the Near East and on the shores of the Mediterranean Sea, where they would storm and plunder. The prophet concentrates on two agonizing questions about the crisis: Can a tyrannical power be overcome by a still greater tyrant? How could the God of right and justice choose such means to further his righteous cause?

The second key concept is related to the word *qedoshi*, "my
Holy One." It expresses the incomparability of God's Being with
all his creation. Yahweh is "wholly other," there is nothing like
him in the created world. Within this conception is the LORD's
all-consuming dreadfulness toward all that is foreign to his Being.
In this sense this idea appears in Isaiah's preaching (cf. Isa. 6;
10:17; 43:15; 49:7). Habakkuk takes over this definition from the
prophetic tradition and gives it a moral setting. This definition
is supported by v. 13, which speaks of "the purity of God's eyes"
which "canst not look on wrong." According to the Law (Lev.
19:2), how can God, who is moral perfection itself and who desires it of his people, how can he "look on faithless men" (v. 13) —
that is the question for the prophet that arises from the crisis.

The third key concept is in the word *tsur*, "Rock," especially
as it occurs quite often in the Psalms. As an image we see in it
steadfastness, continuity, unchangeableness, the motif of protection and security, the foundation of all human confidence and
faith (cf. Deut. 32:4; 2 Sam. 23:3; Ps. 92:16; 31:3; 62:8; 19:15;
62:3). It is a superb expression for a prayerful and trusting awareness. The first two key concepts occur with a possessive suffix;
the last stands without any. The prophet bears witness to the
God who is the holy LORD from of old, the living God, unchangeable in his judgments, consistent in his decisions. Behold,
this is the Lord of the Covenant, the God of the chosen people!

To emphasize this idea and to underline it strongly he varies
the basic text with the words *lo' tamut*, "thou dost not die." In
later years in the *shemoneh 'esreh*, the "Eighteen Benedictions," the
Jewish synagogue employed eighteen verses in its second bene-
diction in praise of Yahweh's Name; so here we are dealing with
the exaltation of the *living* God. A pious scribe seems to have
been shocked that anyone should dare even to suggest about the
ever-living God, "Thou dost not die." So he altered the text, to
turn the prophetic witness into having a human sound about it:
"We shall not die." This textual alteration is one of the *tiqqune
sopherim* (scribal changes) made to express implicitly the prophet's
witness about God; at the same time it fits exactly with his moral
stance, for it guards what is truly human. As he sees the cruelty
of his time, the prophet, bearing witness to his faith, answers
defiantly. Despite the fact that the *rasha'*, the wicked, continue to
pillage passionately, collecting "what is not theirs" with insatiable
greed, subjugating countless multitudes as their prisoners of war,
yet "we shall not die," because the God of life protects his covenant people.

In this connection the prophet's striking historical view appears: Babylonia is "ordained to judgment," *lemishpat,* and "established for chastisement," *lehokiah,* this chosen instrument in God's hands! He *sim,* "sets," "places," and *ysd,* "establishes," "ordains"; these are verbs that express Yahweh's royal prerogative and unsearchable decree. All this the prophet knows well and accepts. For him the agonizing issue is probably this: Why does he who is "of purer eyes than to behold evil," the holy LORD, choose for himself such an instrument to accomplish his will?

That this is a collective complaint, the complaint of the congregation, is seen in its defense of humanity: "Thou art silent when the wicked swallows up the man more righteous than he." The word *hrsh,* "be silent," refers to the behavior of the sovereign, living God, who hides himself in silence and permits the wicked to flourish (cf. 1:2-4).

Verse 14 carries forward this idea and portrays the sovereign LORD as he is in his "work": "Thou makest man." This verse reminds us of creation and of the dignity that mankind received at creation (Gen. 1:26-31; Ps. 8), when his Creator made him lord and set him at the head of the "cosmological pyramid" (P's depiction of creation in Gen. 1:1 – 2:4a). Does God allow man's dignity to be thus defiled? Does he let this humanity, set at the pinnacle of dignity, descend to the level of worms, of "crawling things"? The phrase *lo' moshel bo,* "that have no ruler," brilliantly depicts the helplessness and defenselessness that go with this descent, when there is no one to protect and defend them.

Verse 15 pictures the "wicked" in his cruelty attaining his ends with sadistic delight. The prophet now uses the portrait of a fisherman (*haqqah,* "hook," "harpoon"; *herem,* "fish-net"; *mikmeret,* "drag-net," "trawl"). In this way he pictorializes what helplessness and defenselessness means. The fish, captured in the fisherman's net, wriggles and writhes helplessly, threatened with certain destruction; this is what helpless humanity is like, unable to save himself. The prophet heightens the hopeless situation by showing that there is no one to help. In this hopeless situation people can do nothing but suffer in enforced helplessness. This helpless agony is actually the opposite of the joy of the oppressor, who exults in his success.

Verse 16 describes the events of the prophet's period when the claims of self-divination by the Great Power make themselves evident. It refers back to v. 11b. There the "punitive" power has made its own might its god; here it is the piratical, despoiling instrument, ensuring the "lucrative part" and the "fatty future" for itself—a momentary progression toward success. This prophetic judgment shows how power can be demonized along with the fruits of power.

Verse 17 comes as the conclusion: does power lead only to butchery, cruelty, and brutal exploitation—that is the prophet's question in his agony of mind when, on the one hand he sets forth his complaint, and on the other hand he remains aghast at the absurdity of his time. This is expressed by the words *riq,* "to empty," and *hamal,* "to slaughter without respite," referring to the insatiable nature of the ruthless, with his boundless lawlessness.

Here Habakkuk stands on the side of humanity; in his complaint he appeals to the God of life; he awaits from him protection for mankind in his cruel state of helplessness and exploitation. This pericope expresses most poignantly the humanity of the prophet.

Yahweh's Final Answer (2:1-5)

The LORD replies at last to the prophet, to the complaint he had set forth (1:2-4), to the oracle resulting from it (1:5-11), and to his plea in further response to it (1:12-17). The prophet accepts it in resignation as an adequate answer. In v. 1 the prophet tells us that he will prepare himself, encourage himself, to receive God's command. There follows Yahweh's word, in vv. 3-4, an announcement made in a vision, *hazon,* one that would surely come to pass. With reference to the content of the vision (v. 4) there would be a pronouncement on the matter of the "criminal procedure"—the calling to account and resulting punishment. That leads on to the description in v. 5, while the pericope in vv. 6-20 with its series of woes lists the punishments relating to certain concrete sins.

In v. 1 the prophet encourages himself to perform his prophetic service. He prepares to receive the announcement and to accept it. Till now this "cultic" prophet, representing the congregation, had set forth his issue before God. Now he eagerly awaits to see what the mediating answer will be. The cohortatives of the verbs here, *'e'emodah* and *'etyatstsebah,* express the swelling of his emotions almost to the boiling point: "Let me take my stand on my post, let me just stand on the bastion." In this declaration the prophet expresses his perplexity and bewilderment. In reality he is making a request: "Let me stand along with Thee on the watchtower," or "Do Thou stand along with me on the watchtower" (this is a Hithpael intensive reciprocal form of the verb!). A watchtower was an observatory, a sentry box, where one waited for a *mishmeret,* an announcement. *Matsor* means an earthen mound from which it was the practice to storm a city wall, and so was a fortification, from which one had a good view. It has been suggested that the expression is used in connection with the prophet's storming heaven in prayer. It is difficult to determine when the prophet's words are to be understood in a literal sense and when they have a pictorial sense. We find remarks of this kind elsewhere, as when God calls his human servants to perform his will they retire from before his revelation in order to prepare themselves to accept the declaration (Exod. 33:21; 1 Kgs. 19:11; Mic. 4:14; Ezek. 3:17-18; 33:7-8; Num. 23:3; 24:1). In the case of Habakkuk there may have been in the temple a room, a "clausura," into which the prophet could retreat from the congregation for quiet. There he exercised his prophetic office and could listen to the word of God. On the other hand we could think of the kind of spiritual disposition where he could withdraw into himself, alone with God in his "inner chamber." There he could hear the announcement without distractions and then speak it forth, pure and unadulterated, to the cultic community.

Paying heed from his watchtower Habakkuk watches for, *ʾatsappeh,* the Word, the reality of which he hears in a radical sense; God speaks *in (bi)* him and not just *to* him! This means that the prophet experiences the eternal *dabar* (word) not on the periphery of his being but in his innermost self. It is thus a big problem for him to determine what he should answer in his own defense if he is called to account for his complaints, his argumentativeness. *Tokiah* means to show the right way, to punish, to reprove, to vindicate, to protect, to set free. In his questioning, then, the voice of the cultic prophet presents itself: What should I say to those who have heard my complaint, my representations about the current situation?

In vv. 2-3 we see that his intense concentration, his ardent expectation, have not been in vain. The *hazon* is Yahweh's answer. It is a declaration obtained in an inner vision, conveyed by both sight and hearing. The prophet does not define his unprecedented experience in more detail than to declare the fact that "the LORD answered me." The meaning of the verb *ʿanah* that occurs here is to reply to a question, to give a requisite answer. To begin with God does deal with the content of the judgment he has expressed, but only communicating a command in relationship to it: "Write the vision, make it plain upon tablets, so it may be easy to read" (RSV "so he may run who reads it"). This command means that it is not just this bulletin, as a notice given in general, that is the issue; the content of the events being reported upon is to be regarded as always relevant, since it refers not to present events but to those in the future. *Luah,* the tablet on which one wrote, was used as a means of publicizing news (cf. Isa. 8:1; 30:8).

The appointed time *(moʿed),* the fixed moment for the substantiation of the "vision," is decreed (see "season" in Eccl. 3:1); it was not in man's power but depended on the favor of the sovereign God alone. When he saw fit, then he would fulfill his plan.

The certainty of its near fulfillment is described from various angles and is set before us clearly: "It hastens to the end." *Yapheah* is "panting," "kindling," "gasping for breath," and so it means "indefatigably laboring toward its goal," *qets.* This word expresses the idea that it will in all certainty reach there. It will expend great effort to reach its destination, always moving toward the decreed goal, that is, to fulfillment. God's promise never fails; he does not lie, *kzb.* It draws near resolutely, *boʾ-yaboʾ,* nothing can delay it, *ʾahar;* man must just wait for it attentively in full expectation of its certainty. These varied synonyms all emphasize the one fact — God's declaration, whatever the circumstances, will come to fruition.

Verse 4 is the centerpiece, the heart, of the whole prophecy. The NT quotes it several times (Rom. 1:17; Gal. 3:11; Heb. 10:37). The meaning of the verse is problematical, and text-critical questions arise. There are two elements in it to be brought to the notice of the cultic community. The one is the ethical appraisal of two opposite poles — the *ʿuppelah,* the "puffed up," and the *tsaddiq,* the "righteous." The prophet's characteristic ethical interest becomes apparent here before all else. The LORD who is "of purer eyes" (1:13) and who is "holy" (1:12) well knows his instrument is destined to be punished. He has chosen him in his sovereign manner even if he complains as a person suffering under trial. When God thus decides, it means that he makes a distinction and calls to account. He directs his answer to the complaints that have been uttered (1:2-4, 12-17). The other element is the announcement of judgment that is described as a fate to be fulfilled in the future. Due consideration is to be taken of the process of events, of how life produces its fruits. The "punisher" certainly completes his service, but because of that he makes himself responsible and is bound to be called to account, while the steadfastness of the "righteous" also has its result.

ʿUppelah, a Pual perfect, means "puffed up," full of self-confidence, proud, vain, presumptuous (cf. Num. 14:44; Deut. 1:43). Such characterization fits perfectly with the conceited persons about whom the prophet had something to say at 1:7, 11, 13. The identity of the judgment arises from the way God himself allows his prophet to see the real situation. This is the judgment upon the arrogant Babylonian "Great Power" that is projected into the future; it will be ruined by its success. The German scholar Rudolph interprets this passage by saying that the announcement of judgment is actually in it and so translates by "Man brings about the decreed punishment"; he does so on the basis of a verbal correction to *pe'ullah*, hence meaning an act which carries its punishment (cf. Isa. 65:7). In the same direction Keller seeks to interpret this verse by taking it in the sense of the verb *'alaph*, "faint," "lose consciousness," and so translates by "he decays," "comes to nought." *BHK* suggests altering the word to *hanne'ephal*, "those who are puffed up," "those in whom my [Yahweh's] spirit does not delight," *ratsetah*. This is the LXX's understanding of it, which Elliger supports.

Yashar, "upright," is an expression often found in the Wisdom literature (Ps. 7:1; 11:2; Prov. 2:7; 21:3; Job 4:7; cf. Jer. 18:4; also 2 Sam. 18:4; 1 Kgs. 9:12). It means "upright," "true," "fitting," "suitable," "proper," "reliable," "worthy," "honorable," but not only in a moral sense. It can also indicate the unfortunate result of the above as seen in a real life situation. Therefore the prophet not only indicates a moral defect, but he also brings into view the annihilation of the whole of a person's existence, in that the word *nephesh* (RSV "soul") describes the vital being of a living person. As a result, being "puffed up" brings with it the moral sense that the judgment is a deserved punishment.

This description and the depiction of this fate to be fulfilled in the future has its counterpart: "But the righteous shall live by his faith."

The concept of *tsedaqah*, "righteousness," has a very concentrated content in the OT. Its basic meaning is "communal loyalty," one that goes back to the norms in an existing society. The meaning of *tsedeq* in the case of the chosen people is the covenantal relationship in the Law. Thus the *tsaddiq*, the "devout," is he who corresponds to that norm — he who goes back to the prescriptions of the Law that conform to the expressed will of God and who accepts its binding validity and submits to it wholly.

The term *'emunah* is used here for "faith." In the OT the meaning of the verb *'aman* from which it derives defines its significance. Its usage here is in the verbal form we know as active; deriving from it is its causative and reflective forms, the Hiphil and the Niphal. When it occurs in these forms it shows with special em-

31

phasis that the essence of faith is exhibited in a new situation of
passivity, of steadfastness, endurance, constancy, perseverance,
displayed in the presence of God. A line is to be drawn between
an active and a passive feature of faith. It is God who seizes a
man and enables him (passive) to know the will of the LORD and
to do it (active). With the help of this meaning of the verbal root
it can be determined that, according to the evidence of the OT,
Yahweh "works" faith (Hiphil); man then reflects (Niphal) on
how the dynamic content of the verb *'aman* is apparent, creating
a new situation in his inner being. It activates him to display
that kind of behavior which conforms with the will of God and
which he can receive in submission. Thus it is revealed that faith
is the result of the work of God, and so is a gift.

The *'emunah* (faith) concept displays a concrete content according to the particular meaning of the two verbal forms we
have noted. On the one hand, there arises in a person a new
situation that can be described in terms of passivity — steadfastness, perseverance, resoluteness, staunchness. On the other hand,
the active form of the verb, with reference to this new mode of
behavior, shows that "to believe" means to strengthen yourself in
the revealed word of God, accept it as worthy of belief and so to
trust in it; so to commit yourself to him, and stand alongside
him, convinced that this Other will faithfully stand alongside
you. The verb thus brings together both the passive and the active
aspects of human behavior toward God — confidence, steadfastness, resoluteness, trust, obedience, peace of mind, assurance,
knowing that one is being looked after. So *'emunah* means all these
things.

As expressed in Yahweh's opening declaration, the future of
the two ways of life are drawn with decisive strokes — their end,
their goals, *qets*. The "puffed-upness" manifested against God,
the self-worship and praise of self, these all render evident that
self-deception which discloses humanity's nakedness and so lead
to inescapable judgment. But those who have accepted the guidance of God's will, by their submissive behavior, will inherit the
life to come. This is Yahweh's final answer to the prophet's impatient complaint — the "puffed up" will bear his punishment; the
"righteous," on the other hand, will remain alive amid all his
trials.

Habakkuk's concept of faith is rooted in the prophetic tradition
as we find it in the northern kingdom of Israel, and it is echoed
in the theology of the Elohist and in the preaching of Isaiah the
prophet. The faith of Abraham means that, despite all natural

laws, and despite visible and convincing facts, the LORD gives credence to his Word, and so he "strengthens himself" as he submits himself in that confidence (Gen. 15:5-6; 22:2, 8; E). In this new situation, the LORD's promise, actually through the audacity of faith, becomes the basis on which the future is built. It is on such a foundation that the true possession of life is gained: Abraham became the father of the nations and received back his son as the deposit of the promises.

It was in the period of the Syro-Ephraimitic Wars, actually at their most dangerous moment, that the prophet Isaiah declared: "If you will not believe, surely you shall not be established" (Isa. 7:9). Or again, "Therefore thus says the LORD God, "Behold I am laying in Zion for a foundation, a stone, a tested stone, a precious cornerstone, of a sure foundation': 'He who believes will not be in haste' " (Isa. 28:16). In both cases the existential element becomes apparent, the only criterion for both the community's and the individual's remaining secure. In both cases it is only through faith in the reality of the Covenant that man can continue to be and to live. In Habakkuk's prophecy this existential trait in faith becomes valid. *'Emunah* means both totally trusting behavior and steadfastness alongside God, whose deeds and ways of working remain beyond human comprehension. This is that steadfastness, that persevering behavior alongside the Word of Yahweh and his promise, that in all confidence and trust and in spite of visible facts can look to the God who has spoken and given his promise. Habakkuk witnesses to the power of *'emunah* to resolve crises, in that it opens up a way to the future and guarantees the pledge of life, the certainty of deliverance and preservation. Such is the manner of life of the covenant people, the most conspicuous manifestation of their particular lifestyle.

Verse 5 refers back to v. 4a, deepening its purport. It characterizes more accurately what it means to be "puffed up." It prepares us for the declaration repeated throughout vv. 6-20 that begins in each case with the word "Woe."

Habakkuk's basic theology comes to the fore here: the activities of the threatening Great Power that is acting for the LORD are only temporary — their deeds will not remain unpunished. Their accountability will not depart even though it tarries. The prophet's unbroken view is shown in the expression *we'aph ki,* "how much more," "truly it will be that. . . ." Yet difficulties arise in understanding the verse. The usual translation is: "Truly, wine is treacherous," *hayyayin boged,* or in the comparative sense: "Wine does not let you down as much as being 'puffed up' deceives

33

you." The man who worships himself (offers incense to himself)
loses the ability of self-criticism, and so the ability to find his
bearings, now that his sense of proportion has fallen to pieces.
He can no longer see clearly; he cannot make objective judgments
in the affairs of his life. How much more is this so when wine
makes you intoxicated. According to the prophet Hosea's judgment, "Wine and new wine take away the understanding" (or,
"rob a man of his heart" [i.e., his brains, in the original Hungarian text]; Hos. 4:11). The heart is the center of a person's life
where his thoughts, decisions, feelings, and impulses all find their
birth. Such self-deception and delusion is a recipe for resulting
destruction. That this verse applies to the Babylonians actually
even supports this view. For the Babylonian court and its courtiers (Dan. 5) provide us with a historical record of their fame
for being great drinkers. The Dead Sea Scroll text of Habakkuk
(1QpHab) has a variant reading. It reads *hon,* "goods," "wealth,"
instead of *yayin.* Wealth falsely acquired, that is, goods seized by
force, are indefensible. Such conceited people the prophet calls
geber yahir, "arrogant man." He knows no rest because of his
violence and drunkenness; for despite his successes naturally he
has no future, for he can never reach his goal.

Verse 5b lays bare the insatiable greed of conceited, arrogant
persons, displaying it as it applies to the boundless grasping lust
of the Babylonians. The prophet uses three pictures to describe
this:

(a) They greedily open wide their throat (cf. RSV "His greed
is as wide as Sheol"). The word *nephesh* here means "throat," "the
digestive canal," the "seat" of all desires and appetites. The RSV
translation simply identifies the insatiable greed of the arrogant
man with his wide-open throat, which like death or Sheol, "never
has enough."

(b) "Like death he has never enough." *Sb'* means "fill up,"
"feel satisfied," "have enough to eat," "feel contented." It serves
to describe both greed and insatiability.

(c) "He gathers for himself all nations, and collects as his own
all peoples." *'Asaph* means "assemble," "carry to one place," as
in the autumn one gathers in the harvest. *Qbts* means "collect,"
"gather together." He is picturing their advance, conquest, and
amassing of booty in their lust for power.

After this description there follows in v. 6 a daring turning
point that forms a bridge to the following pericope. "All these" —
are they the haughty plunderers, or are they the objects of the
mockery and laughter? This concept of an eye for an eye has

appeared already, the announcement of the punishment that fits
the crime about which the following pericope speaks in detail.
Mashal means "proverb," "comparison," "parable"; *melitsah*, "a
satire," "a song of mockery"; *hidah* is "a secret," "a riddle," "a
speech containing a hidden meaning."

Bit by bit the final destruction is shown to be unavoidable. He
who has caused complete destruction, he who has plundered,
humiliated, ravished, brought sorrow and suffering will share in
a like affliction. It will be worse than affliction of body and soul.
Not only does he picture them helplessly compelled to witness
the destruction of the treasures they have collected; they will have
to listen to scorn and mockery from those whom they have oppressed and made to suffer in humiliation.

Dirge over the Doomed Tyrant (2:6-20)

After the condensed presentation in v. 5 there follows a dirge that
reviews the fate of the doomed tyrant in the judgment to be fulfilled in the days to come. This "vision," *hazon*, expresses the
other pole to the "five woes" construction; it seals the fate of the
ruthless Great Power, the Babylonians.

In its form this pericope is a speech declaring a prophetic
judgment, rather as if it were composed of a mosaic of little pieces
of prophetic utterances. It is apparent that here too we meet with
a description of concrete sins about which the announcement of
judgment is also completely concrete. The whole sentence is defined as seen from the angle of the prophet's moral stance, so that
judgment flows therefrom. This moral stance is the ruling motif
that sounds throughout the whole dirge.

The first four "woes" make public the bill of indictment upon
the sins that have been committed and the announcement of the
judgment that is to be meted out (2:6b-17). The fifth "woe" does
not contain any preamble or announcement of judgment. This is
because we find a description that carries the judgment within
it.

Each paragraph begins with the word *hoy!* (woe to), which
occurs in a wailing lament for the dead. It indicates that death
is near or has actually come, that the punishment is inevitable.
Along with the naming of the actual sin and the announcement
of the appropriate punishment, the judgment is apparent in terms
of the *lex talionis*, "an eye for an eye." This means that the evildoer
will be subject to the evil he has done. "The measure you give
will be the measure you get" (Matt. 7:2) on the day of judgment.
The sinner must taste the pain his sin has caused. One way of

shaping the punishment is for the sinner to bear the load of his sin and to suffer the fate that he has brought upon others.

This pericope as we have it has no doubt resulted from redactional work done upon it as a result of the Exile. Verse 13, for example, reminds us of the ideas we meet with in Jer. 51:58, which deals with the same judgment meted out to the Great Power of that day. Likewise the motif of messianic prediction that arose in a later period (Isa. 11:9) turns up in v. 14. In the same way v. 8b, which v. 17 expounds in detail, is to be regarded as a later insertion. Here the editor incorporates the destruction of the cedars of Lebanon among the list of sins he attributes to a tyrant.

In the mosaic buildup of the pericope, the prophet Habakkuk's theological concepts are expressed in the form of a song of lament for the dead; at the same time, on the basis of his theological point of view, the lament is connected with the dialogue in ch. 1 between the LORD and his prophet; and it expresses proof that the Lord has listened to his prophet.

The pronouncement of judgment expressed in the five "woes" refers back to v. 5b. The little peoples, among them Judah, who had been subjugated by the Babylonians will utter this dirge for the dead. Yahweh had maintained the Babylonians as his instrument of punishment. But after the completion of this commission they would be accounted responsible for their behavior so that they would have to accept their punishment.

Woe to the Plunderers! (2:6b-8) What has become a passionate lust for possession and an unjust appropriation of material goods is adjudged in this paragraph. The contents are described in an expressive picture: the greedy, grabbing Great Power, after reaching an unquenchable passion, appears as a helpless beggar. His creditors rebel against him, he bleeds to death, he is himself despoiled and becomes totally their prey. The participle *hammarbeh*, from the Hiphil of *rbh*, means "multiplying," "increasing"; the grammatical form shows it means "the more he has, the more he must have, and he never has enough." The prophetic critic passes judgment not only on the heaping up of material possessions, and on how these have been obtained through injustice; he also objects to the lawless, violent confiscation of another's goods: "He heaps up what is not his own." We find him using a pun here, *lo'-lo* (lit. "not his"; cf. 1:6). Are there any bounds to such passion? When will the end of it be? asks the prophet.

The desire to possess appears in another form when one pawns one's material goods. When a creditor secures a deposit and then asks for it back from his debtor he only gains for himself a further worry in the preservation of his goods. The term *ʿabtit* is a *hapax legomenon*, that is, it occurs only here. It apparently means a pledge, taking something as security. The exact definition of what this means here is not given. Perhaps we can think of conquered peoples having to pay a war indemnity or being taxed as vassals. This can grow to be an unbearable burden on little nations, among them Judah. According to our prophet's picture the Great Power itself will become the overburdened people, finding it impossible to bear the confiscation of its goods and pay the indemnity imposed upon it, as atonement to those whom it has first exploited.

The punishment will be sudden, unexpected, no one counting on it. *Petaʿ* means "all of a sudden," "in the blink of an eye," when those who have been exploited will "arise" and will demand indemnity for their goods. They will sting like poisonous snakes *(nshk)*, they will bite like wild beasts forced into a cage; once they are released they will tear their captors to pieces. The content of this ghastly picture is deepened by the use of the participle *mezaʿzeʿeka*, from the root *zwʿ*, meaning "arouse," "startle." It describes the assault of an animal that had seemed to be dead but that, wild with pain, seizes its prey and slaughters it. It means that those who had been oppressed and tormented out of their wits had been able to gather their strength together and rush upon their tormentors, who, unable to escape, fell victim to them. The *lex talionis* means that he who has been robbed and plundered will now himself do the plundering. The word *mesh-issah* here means plunder, prey, booty, implying total destruction.

The reason for this example of "an eye for an eye" is given in v. 8: "Because you have plundered many nations, all the remnant of the peoples shall plunder you." The verb *shalal* means rob, extort, exploit. So the treatment is to be one of retaliation. The "remnant," *yeter*, the survivors, will behave in the same way. All this is not just the consequence of their behavior; the LORD has done it in the service of his justice, for he does not leave a sin unpunished. The verse refers back to v. 4, to the pronouncing of judgment upon the "puffed up."

The second half of the verse has a moral content, for with the preservation of human life the total judgment upon the oppressing Great Power becomes evident.

Woe to the House Built upon Plunder! *(2:9-11)* He who wants
to ensure his own future prosperity and that of his family by
means of plunder cannot avoid the judgment. The "house," *bet*,
means not just the family home but those who live in it too, even
the children. While the previous "woe" envisioned the accumulation of goods obtained by plunder, now these serve to ensure
the family's future security and that of his descendants. *Betsa*᷾
covers property gained by injustice and by plunder. The related
verb *batsa*᷾ means to commit burglary, to seize unlawful gain.

In the picture the nests "set on high" illustrate the idea of
being totally unapproachable and of the effort required to seek
for security. He who has collected his goods by violence, who has
robbed and exploited, now seeks to secure his "valuables" along
with his household for the days to come. He lives in a continual
state of fear, not so much that he should lose his acquisitions but
the advantages he gains from them. So he flees to an unreachable
height, in order to gain protection there, and in this way to "sneak
out" from the hand of the avenger. *Ntsl* means "slip out," "crawl,"
"extricate oneself," "escape," "go out," "set free." We do not need
to give a mythological meaning to the verse, nor do we need to
see in it any suggestion of protecting oneself from the gods who
dwell on the hilltops or of recourse to them. On the Babylonian
scene the mighty stone walls built high expressed an attempt at
protection and at securing safety. This provision for the future
remained only a futile endeavor, for not only did it produce no
result, it did not even ensure any protection. The whole exercise
was an outrageous delusion.

Ya᷾*ats boshet:* "You have devised shame to your house." Your
cunningly thought-out plan will meet with disappointment, it will
not succeed; innocent blood sticks to it — the extermination of
many a nation, the extinguishing of innocent lives. Security at
the cost of innocent lives can offer neither protection nor a foundation for future generations. The tyrant who expels peoples with
violence, seizing their possessions for himself, has in reality not
enriched himself at all, nor has he ensured his future; he has
actually sinned against himself and has turned himself into a
criminal. The definition of sin as *het*᷾ expresses the idea of losing
one's direction; it describes deviating from the proper road, resulting in destruction and annihilation.

The particle *ki*, "for," not only gives the reason for the inevitable judgment as retribution for sin but also points to the undeniable existence of the *corpus delicti*. The latter makes the
indictment that renders the sin undeniable. The stones used as

building material for the "house," erected as it has been out of wicked acquisitions, will "cry out," $z^e q$. Whereupon "the beam from the woodwork" will answer back, $^e nh$. They will charge that the building was an act of unrighteousness or a shameful plan that was an outrageous scheme. The "house" that had been built from stolen material, which ought to have given protection and ensured the safety of the next generation, will actually cry out accusingly in its very component parts, thereby betraying its wicked origin. It was not just dumb elements like wood and stone that made this accusation before God; its builder brought shame upon his family before the eyes of the community of nations.

In the case of Babylonia we possess historical documents that show how, after Nebuchadnezzar's death in 562, the whole empire began to fall to pieces, and how its final collapse took place two years later under his son, Amel-Marduk (OT Evil-Merodach). Throughout the following four decades there was not one ruler with sufficient stamina to maintain the once powerful empire or ensure its future well-being. Because of the religious and political rupture, it started on a decline that nothing could withstand. Largely responsible for this was its last ruler, Nabonaid (Nabonidus), who broke from the worship of Marduk and served the moon-god of Haran. Thus he came into conflict with both the priests and the people as a whole. It is understandable, then, that when the Persians, in a succession of attacks, besieged the capital city, despite its stone walls it turned out to be defenseless, for no one took the side of the king. In 539 Babylon fell without a blow, despite possessing a regular defense system, and was forced to surrender before the troops of Cyrus.

Woe to Those Who Build a Town with Blood! (2:12-14) The work of a glossator shows itself in this section, as editor of vv. 13a and 14. This cry of "Woe" is short. Verse 12 pronounces the deed worthy of judgment, while v. 13b pronounces the judgment on the attempt to be unsuccessful and ineffectual. So now comes the judgment upon the ambitious conqueror, who by sustained plundering has sought fame and glory for himself.

We should note the relationship with the previous section. The difference is that there, as he looks to the future, the aim of the "puffed up" is to acquire security for the individual and for his family through stolen goods; but here the aim is to create renown and glory for the days to come by building with blood. The prophet's picture of the conqueror's horrendous activities shows that the latter makes use of the blood that maintains human life

39

to advertise his own renown. Any building that arises at the cost
of blood means the massacring of an enslaved people, or the
severe pillaging that a conqueror imposes upon the conquered.
The term *'awlah* means "injustice," "lawlessness," "terror." The
accusation is that it enhances the value of cities and their battlements if the conqueror has not shrunk from all kinds of intrigue
and unlawful activities along with the shedding of innocent blood.
They had known no consideration, no fair-mindedness, no pity
when it was a question of gaining their ends. This observation
can also mean that in subjugating others the conquerors in their
turn will be subjugated, forcibly deprived of those goods with
which they had built up their strength. It could refer to prisoners
of war or slaves doing forced labor, not an uncommon sight in
our prophet's time. Historical records, and especially a series of
archeological excavations, now show us Nebuchadnezzar's most
magnificent and stupendous edifices in ruins, especially in the
capital city.

The judgment ends by declaring that all exertion (*yg'* and *y'ph*
mean exhausting and sweaty work) will end up as merely booty
to be burned *(bede 'esh)*, will produce no results, but will be just
vanity *(bede riq)*. All this will come about not from fate but from
the will of the LORD, whose judgment is revealed in this way in
historical events.

Verse 14 is an insertion; it does not contain any reasons, but
speaks of the wideness of the knowledge of the glory of the LORD.
The earth is full of it, so his power becomes evident in that he
keeps his finger on the pulse of history and directs all things in
sovereign style.

Woe to the Lechers! (2:15-17) When, in positions of power,
people lay hold of the good life, they can sink deep into a moral
slough. On such persons in power, who have become crazed with
drink and so have insulted the human dignity of their fellows, the
prophet declares judgment. It is here that we get a glimpse into
a forceful person's interior private life. Debauchery and drunken
orgies that know no bounds are one way to reveal what the good
life and success can lead to. In such a situation the "big shot,"
in giving a party, goes to excess and ensures that his guests
become drunk. He gets them to discard their clothes and rape
one another. The word *hemah* means excitement, anger, erotic
passion, sexual stimulation. Here we have a prophetic judgment
upon demoralization. The drunken man becomes a victim because he is robbed of his power of action and so becomes con-

quered. Through the prophet God calls it a sin on the part of the "conqueror" if he hurts a fellow human being *(rea')* in the area of his human dignity. The judgment then is this: *your* repute, *your* human dignity, will be shamed. In terms of an eye for an eye this means that if by deceitful means you rob your neighbor of his human dignity and bring contempt upon him, a similar fate will be yours. He pictorializes the judgment then in this expressive way — you will have to drink the cup of the LORD's wrath, "and shame will come upon your glory."

Verse 17 is an insertion referring back to v. 8b. It adds to the previous list of sins and expresses all the more need for the punishment that they have earned. The senseless destruction of the cedars of Lebanon is an aspect of ruthless violence. What is in question by the prophet is the unintelligent chopping down of beautiful trees to build palaces to the glory of the builders. In Israelite tradition, in its Wisdom literature, and particularly in the poems of the Psalter, the forests of Lebanon were planted by the hand of Yahweh (Ps. 104:16; 80:1), and they proclaim the might of the Creator. Wanton violence therefore dare not declare war on him — that would be insanity — or on his plant or animal world. Such violent acts "plunge you into mourning" (rather than RSV "terrify you"); the judgment and the destruction therefore are inescapable. Rudolph refers to the Neo-Babylonian Chronicles which describe this very destruction that Nebuchadnezzar brought upon the territories of Syria-Palestine when he claimed rule over the land of Lebanon.

Woe to the Idolators! *(2:18-19)* This "Woe" is from the hand of a later editor. He has added it into the list of "Woes" as number five under the influence of the previous ones. It is possible that the prophet himself connected it with the previous ones as a witness in the form of a profession of faith in the only true God. It is remarkable that the cry of *hoy* does not open the declaration as in the previous "woes," along with the consequent declarations of judgment to follow. What we find is something rooted in Israel's ancient tradition, a witness to what the Decalogue has to say about God. It is that God in his actions is the living, mighty LORD, the God of life, *'el hay.* Beside him every divinity is born of human fantasy or is the product of human hands. Mention is made here of divinities whittled from wood or of statues of poured metal *(pesel, massekah).* Defense of Yahweh as the sole Ruler resounds in the prophet's question: "What profit is a dumb piece of carving, or a metal alloy that human beings have fashioned?

Can these be of any use?" They could only impart a false Torah
since they do not understand Yahweh's revelation; there is no
ruah, "breath," in them. So there is a double judgment made here
upon the uselessness and the ineffectualness of idolatry. An idol
cannot help one in times of trouble and can give no guidance in
days of perplexity. It follows then that the idolator is left to himself, without prop or stay. It is God alone who can uphold and
guide, the God who is alive! The apathetic idol-gods are dumb
and helpless. Yahweh, the living God, in his own might can act
in every situation. Israel's God is the living God! Consequently
in this verse the prophet brings up basic questions about witnessing to God. It is true that the announcement of judgment
and reasons for it are missing, but the person under judgment
bears the judgment within himself.

Verse 20 is an independent "inlay" in the mosaic. It refers back
directly to the preceding verse, to the helplessness of idols over
against Yahweh's appearance in the temple as the living and present Lord, before whom all people in the whole of creation must
keep silence. *Has* ("Silence!") is a cultic formula, calling for silence and reverence and for an expression of respectful allegiance.
It reflects the cry of "Woe" as well: "Behold, all will be fulfilled
of which the judgment has spoken, because there is *ruah* in him
who announced it, and this can bring to its conclusion the judgment uttered with enlivening strength and power." This LORD is
"holy," therefore he is wholly "other" than the created world. He
is to be feared and he is absolutely unapproachable; yet as the
God who is present he is present in his temple! Before him one
can but bow down and worship in fear and trembling, yet in
childlike trust. In this way, then, v. 20 forms the link, the "bridge"
to ch. 3, to the prophet's prayer, uttered as a hymn for public
worship in response to the theophany, the "appearing" of God.

YAHWEH'S ARRIVAL (3:1-19)

The text of ch. 3 is in poor condition, yet in it we reach the
highlight of Habakkuk's prophecy. In this remarkable prayer we
are given news of the theophany of the LORD as he arrives. The
prophet's agonizing questionings subside, because he both sees
and hears the coming of his God, who comes to administer justice. With the overcoming of the "wicked" he sets his people free.
Out of this terrible experience a prayer rises to his lips, in which
he extols his mighty LORD in a voice of fear and joy.

In both form and content this prayer differs from the two

previous chapters. In these Yahweh and his prophet had carried on a dialogue in the form of complaint alternating with oracle, where God's sovereignty and judgment became apparent with a declaration through a *massa*', "oracle." Here, in lyric verse applicable to public worship, ch. 3 describes a theophany as the prophet preaches a sermon in the shape of a hymn composed of an amalgam of elements. As such it is unparalleled; in it the prophet extols the LORD who is arriving to fight and to conquer.

It is noteworthy that this chapter carries a separate heading (3:1). In the chapter we find evidences of its use as a prayer for public worship (3:3, 9, 13). Its conclusion at 3:19b makes reference to its musically liturgical nature. These technical musical notices form a later insertion. They allow us to conclude that this chapter, this prophetic installment, is an independent prayer. It could be used in the cult at a time when the enemy was at the gate or at the failure of a harvest or when there was a cattle plague (v. 17). It is possible that the unknown "choirmaster" was the author himself; this would explain why he placed his hymn among the temple songs, as 3:19 implies. From a practical point of view he himself saw to the supplying of the necessary musical score so as to make sure it would be easily accessible in the hymnbook (elements of the Psalter?) used in public worship.

This prayer consists of various elements. Apart from elements of hymnic praise, we find in it, both visually and audibly experienced, motifs of a theophany as reported by the prophet. There are also mythological elements that Israel had learned from being in touch with the surrounding peoples. Israel had taken these over and had built them into its monotheistic faith and so was enabled to see Yahweh's deeds through his eyes.

Some scholars suggest that, even as he "saw" this mythological theophany, the prophet constructed his own vision and audition to help him understand it. Others see in it qualities of an eschatological hymn or the pictorializing of a religious experience. Still others suggest it might be a personal experience reflecting back to 2:1-4 as an accompaniment to a prophetic liturgy.

Added to these suggestions made by some German OT scholars are those of W. F. Albright ("The Psalm of Habakkuk," in *Studies in Old Testament Prophecy Presented to T. H. Robinson*, 1-18). He sees in ch. 3 a multiple web, an amalgam of motifs from Canaanite poems applied to Yahwism with elements of an ancient Israelite theophany. It could have arisen from the time of one of Israel's kings and been taken over as a prophet's sermon by a contemporary or earlier prophet. J. E. Eaton ("The Origin and

Meaning of Habakkuk 3," *ZAW* 76 [1964] 144-71) finds a cultic element in it that would fit with the autumn festival, when Israel celebrated Yahweh's triumph over the powers of chaos and infertility. It is fitting that we should pursue inquiry into the interrelationships within the whole prophecy, and so avoid any one-sided generalization.

The central theme of ch. 3 is the prophet's witness to the theophany of Yahweh, one that he experienced through both eye and ear. Habakkuk's God is the incomprehensibly silent One, the LORD who is present in the temple (2:20), who suddenly steps forth out of his silence and makes war for the liberation of his people. Standing on his watchtower (2:1-4), the prophet had received a report about the "puffed up" Great Power, Babylonia, with respect to its coming fate. Now he witnesses visually and audibly the fulfillment of that judgment.

The prophet begins and ends his description of the Yahweh-theophany with his own personal experience (3:2, 16). It initiates his first prayer and supports the second as a hope for the future.

There are two main sections to the prophet's vision of the LORD's appearance, and these are connected with the introduction and the conclusion respectively. The division of the text is as follows:

1. Introduction: invocation, the prophet's presentation of his request, v. 2

2. Description of the LORD's arrival, vv. 3-7

3. Description of the LORD's battle and victory, vv. 8-15

4. The prophet's response: horror, joy, trust, vv. 16, 18-19, (17)

The first verse of ch. 3 contains a heading. It informs us of the prophet's name, and accentuates how, as in 1:1, Habakkuk is in fact a prophet, *nabi'*. The editor classifies this chapter as a prayer, *tephillah,* one that expounds the complaint or request; yet within it there sounds the motif of intervention (Ps. 17:1; 86:1; 90:1; 102:1; 109:4; 142:1). It is probable that, because of the complaints sounded in ch. 1, the editor makes use of this designation and strengthens the idea that Habakkuk, as a cultic prophet, intervened on behalf of his people.

The meaning of the musical term *Shigionoth* is unclear. The LXX translates it by *meta odes,* "with a song," as its comment on the verse, while the Latin Vulgate translates by *pro ignorantis,* "not understood"! Taking into account the form and contents, we can understand by this obscure term a verse-form in which not only the rhythm rambles but so also does the versifier, in the mood of one offering prayer and under the influence of his experience.

Introduction: Invocation, the Prophet's Presentation of His Request (3:2)

This verse introduces the theophany that contains the prophet's prayer. There are two motifs in this invocation: information on the prophet's experience of horror, and a description of his plea.

The prophet refers back to 2:1-4. Standing on his watchtower he had heard the report of Yahweh. Now he expands on what he heard, for he had now grasped it, had thought through this report, this communication in which God had revealed his will. The term *shema͑*, "heard," refers to this communication; it means a report conveyed by word. The LORD had spoken, and the prophet had heard him. The content of this report which God had spoken concerned the execution of his judgment. What the prophet hears about the LORD's future "work" *(po͑al)* fills him with fear and horror. The verb *yare͗*, "fear, be appalled," shows the human reaction when experiencing God's nearness.

The request he makes is that Yahweh should fulfill all that he had laid before his prophet by sight and by hearing. This request shows once again Habakkuk's typical features as he bears witness to God. The prophet's God, seemingly dumb and helpless over against the idol-divinities (2:19), is actually the living, active LORD, whose power could bring to fruition his acts based on his eternal plans. This is what the request *hayyehu*, "bring it [i.e., "thy work," *pa͑alka*] to life" (RSV "renew it"), refers to. The prophet's insistent request is that God should intervene as soon as possible in the current critical events and rectify them as soon as he can. The words *beqereb shanim*, "in the midst of the years," refer to the near future, that is, it will be made manifest (following the LXX and reading the Niphal *tiwwada͑* for MT Hiphil *todia͑;* see *BHS*) to everyone when the LORD works his righteous judgment. By this the prophet holds before his eyes the great events of salvation history. These all brought great changes in the life of the chosen people, and they apply now as he interprets the crisis of his time. In 2:3 Yahweh had spoken of the "appointed time" *(mo͑ed)*, hidden indeed from mankind, but a time that would be proved true, being dependent on God alone. It is to this that the prophet now refers and urges the approach of this decisive moment. To bear this "moment" with all its significance mankind needs God's mercy. That is why the prophet requests "in wrath remember mercy." The term *rogez* means "wrath," "the heat of passion," as when a man shakes with anger. The noun *raham* ("mercy") speaks of the anxious solicitation of parents toward their children (*rehem* is "womb"!), and so of compassionate love. These anthropomorphic and anthropopathic pictures bring the Being of God all the closer to us. In his prayer the prophet not only sets forth his request, he also bears witness to his God as the living, powerfully active, dreadful but compassionate LORD, the God who redeems his people. Habakkuk's God is the mighty LORD who directs history, the gentle, loving Father of his people!

It is to this request that the theophany comes in answer (3:3-15) — Yahweh arrives and renews his work, "brings it to life," "in the midst of the years."

Description of the LORD's Arrival (3:3-7)

Habakkuk's vision is rooted in Israel's historical past. We find motifs here to remind us of the decisive chapters in the history of salvation. We saw in chs. 1 and 2 how well the prophet could use the shape of the psalms of complaint to express himself (1:2-4, 12-17). Here we have the conviction also that he was well versed in the past history of the chosen people and knew their traditions. Consequently the basic elements of the theophany are woven together from historical material. For example, we can find a relationship with the Song of Deborah (Judg. 5), with the hymnic praise of Moses (Exod. 15; Deut. 32, and in part, 33), with the wilderness wanderings, with several episodes in the Sinai proclamation (Exod. 16–17; Num. 21–25; Josh. 3:10 in part) and with the motifs of several historical psalms (Pss. 68, 95, 107, 136). All this reveals the source of the chosen people's faith, namely, the LORD's saving acts. These had led to a recognition of God's Covenant and had caused prayers of praise and glory to spring up out of Israel's heart. All was thanksgiving, all was praise — each an echo, an answer, to acts of grace. These were a living sign that they had really grasped the LORD's life-sustaining acts and had understood them as such. Since Yahweh's acts were acts of redemption and the doing of them belonged organically to his holy Being, the recognizable symbol of Israel's way of life was ceaseless praise, exalting the God of their salvation. They were expressing thereby that he truly lives (Isa. 38:17-19; Ps. 78:4).

The prophet sees the LORD as he who is coming from Teman, arriving from Mt. Paran (v. 3). The emphasis made here is that Yahweh is coming from the Sinai Peninsula, heading straight northward, crossing over the territory of Edom to arrive at Judah.

Paran, on the Sinai Peninsula, lay in the area around Mt. Sinai. It can be identified with the highlands known today as Jebel Faran, some 80 kilometers (50 miles) to the west of Petra. Teman is in the land of Edom, the name being that of a sub-tribe or of its capital (cf. Amos 1:12). It occurs in the Song of Deborah (Judg. 5:4) and in the Song of Moses (Deut. 32:2). These names preserve remains of ancient myths, elements in ancient theophanies, which describe God as the mountain-dwelling LORD. This was the route by which Yahweh long before had arrived to set his people free from their Egyptian bondage in order to conclude a covenant with them. Elijah too traveled by this route when in great despair on reaching Mt. Horeb he complained about the smashed altars and the broken covenant; but it was then that he heard the LORD, in a "still, small voice," renewing his mission in his plan for the future (1 Kgs. 19:3-21).

Yahweh strides into these "eternal ways" (v. 6, RSV "his ways were as of old") and thus appears before his people. The prophet is emphasizing the idea of identity and of continuity. He is the God of the fathers who had revealed himself to Moses, who had made a covenant, who had chosen Israel alone out of all the peoples of the earth and had bound them into the service of his plan of salvation. This then was he who was now arriving, who was at work marvelously in history, in order to confront his enemies and grant release to his people. Habakkuk is the prophet of God, the mighty LORD of the story of salvation. God's ancient name, *'eloah*, stands here in the text, giving a powerful emphasis to the contents of v. 3. The same form of the divine name stands in the Song of Moses (Deut. 32:15) to declare him to be the Creator of the universe. Then there is the most explicit definition of God, *qadosh*, holy, absolutely other than the profane world, utterly unapproachable and wholly to be feared (cf. 1:12). With these words the prophet reviews the power and sublimity of the LORD's character, and at the same time justifies the staggering experience of the power of the LORD that has shaken his humanity (3:2, 16).

His presence is hidden by a terrible brilliance and radiance, making the LORD invisible to mankind (v. 4). *Nogah* means a stream of light, as when the sun pours forth its countless rays at which a mere human being is unable to look. This brilliance produces radiant light *('or)*, flashing from his hand *(miyyado)*, emerging like the horns of a stag *(qarnayim)*. A stag is a symbol of power, of might. God cannot be described in human language either in his being or in his might; man can only experience him.

47

This is what the prophet (or, as some suppose, an interpretative editor) refers to when at 3:4b he inserted as his witness that behind the blinding rays God, for mankind's sake, remains in his incomprehensible hiddenness; for that is where God's power is actually to be found. As far as man can see this is a cloak that covers and hides Yahweh's mysterious Being and the power that directs his acts. In the history of their call and mission the prophets Isaiah and Ezekiel shared similar terrifying experiences (Isa. 6; Ezek. 1–3).

This majestic glory *(hod)* of the LORD as he arrives covers the heavens *(shamayim)*, prompting the earth to manifestations of praise. This is how they magnify the Creator LORD, the visible and the invisible world humbly giving honor to the God of life and the Lord of history. In this witness by the prophet the features of creator *(bore')* and of savior *(moshia͑)* merge together in the person of the God who is Israel's covenantal God.

In v. 3 (as also in vv. 9, 13) the musical sign *selah* is found. It may mean "a call to sustain a pause," "repeat!," "change the key!"; or it may be instructions about doing obeisance, given by the choirmaster to the congregation. Since this word stands after the announcement of the LORD's arrival, it could signal the idea of "Forte!" or "Sound loud the trumpets" before the LORD! By means of this sign the later editor sought to give special emphasis to the prophet's words.

This LORD who is present in his royal majesty arrives with an accompaniment. His herald is pestilence, while plague *(deber,* feverish heat, burning flames) is his rearguard. These "envoys" appear in person, for those who travel in his embassy arrive for judgment. This personification refers back to the demonic forces in the ancient Canaanite religion, to the power of those horrible divinities that oppressed mortal human beings with epidemics or with destructive droughts (perhaps meaning burning fevers). According to the prophet's vision these horrible demons have no independent sphere of influence but are inferior beings who stand to serve Yahweh just as does the punitive Great Power, Babylonia. Here we have a reference to the story of salvation, that is, to the period of the ten plagues in Egypt when with the murderous pestilence Pharaoh's heart was hardened (Exod. 9:7); in this way God prepared the way of deliverance. Thus pestilence was then an instrument of judgment, and becomes so here in Yahweh's hand.

Verse 6 pictures a general leading his troops on to the field of battle; he takes up his stance and allots his army their places in the line of combat. The verb ⁽amad means to go to the front, while *madad* is to survey the scene of action, the field of battle. Nothing escapes his survey or evades his notice. These are expressive anthropomorphic images. They describe acutely the movement of troops, their forward momentum.

Verse 6 goes on to show the reaction of the created earth and of humanity to the manifestation. The Creator of the universe is present in the person of its Commander-in-Chief. At a mere glance from him *(r²h)* the nations leap up *(ntr)* in fear (following the LXX reading; not as RSV "he shook"). This situation can be compared to sudden danger befalling a person, reaching him completely unexpectedly; he then flees frantically, screaming, only to find the whole circle closed. So he falls as their prey.

This fearful manifestation shakes not only mankind, however, but also the mountains, symbols of permanency and steadfastness. Even the hills are scattered and their stability called into question. The words here *gibe⁽ot*, ⁽*olam*, and *harere ⁽ad* mark the oldest and most stable parts of the earth according to the conception of prayerful piety (cf. Ps. 90:2; Prov. 8:25; Job 15:7). But now those stable and unchangeable areas, basic elements in the whole world, crumble to pieces, turn to dust, "sink low," are annihilated *(puts)* (cf. Mic. 1:4; Nah. 1:5). As against this "his [God's] paths are everlasting!"

The prophet has turned his eyes once again to the great events of salvation history: the LORD had gone before his people through the Red Sea, in the wilderness, and at Mt. Sinai. He had always come, and with his arrival his people had received liberation.

The verse has a mythological setting rooted in Israel's Exodus tradition. The same picture is evident in the Song of Deborah, which speaks of the mountains quaking and crumbling to dust (Judg. 5:5). The same manifestation accompanied God when he came forth from Seir and marched "from the region of Edom." Behind this image there exists an actual geological natural phenomenon. This is the earth fracture which runs from Lebanon in the north, between Anti-Lebanon and Hermon, then southwest through the Jordan Valley and the Dead Sea, and on down to the land of Edom. The explanation given in the mythologies, the earliest traces of which are at the Exodus and in the Song of Deborah, and what we read here, is that it was connected with the movements of the gods. So these are ancient motifs in this theophany. The prophet, however, has demythologized this ancient notion and employed it for the history of God's saving work.

While v. 6 generally alludes to the shaking of the nations when the LORD manifests himself, v. 7 defines the areas more closely. It alludes to the inhabited areas of Cushan and Midian, those habitable areas nearest to Sinai on the Arabian steppes close by the Red Sea. The prophet thus sees that "the tents of Cushan stand under judgment" *(tahat 'awen ra'iti 'ohole kushan)*, "and the curtains of the land of Midian tremble." The text is irretrievably damaged, however, leaving us with problems of interpretation. Nevertheless, seen in connection with the preceding verses, this verse means the dismay of the region's inhabitants at the mere manifestation of the LORD as he arrives for judgment.

Description of the LORD's Battle and Victory (3:8-15)

This section marks the decisive turning point of the theophany, expressing as it does its central idea: Yahweh has arrived as Commander-in-Chief equipped for war, and he engages in battle victoriously.

The first part of the theophany (3:3-7) had described in written form how the LORD would arrive in the majesty of his might and in the fearfulness of his nature. It is not only the prophet who would be dismayed in his whole being — it would be the whole created world. This sequence of thought is shown by a change of the verbs from perfect to imperfect forms, indicating that we have reached the fulfillment of events. For in this section we meet with a new style of writing, that of a poetic address. The many-colored vortex of the accumulation of events and the prophet's gradually developing inner tension explain the change of style in the theophany and point to the extraordinary listing of events with an intensity reflected from the previous description.

As we read through v. 8 we notice that the theophany is in two main parts. Under the influence of his experience of the vision, words had congealed on the prophet's lips; now he seeks to break out from this numbing situation. In seeking to request an explanation of this bewildering situation he turns to God: "Was thy wrath against the rivers, O LORD? Was thy anger against the rivers, or thy indignation against the sea, when thou didst ride upon thy horses, upon thy chariot of victory?"

The prophet's question therefore is not simply a rhetorical question, such as was used in the poetry of hymns and to which no answer was expected. Habakkuk's question was born under the stress of his ghastly experience, when the seer is really questioning in himself and seeking to explain the peculiar situation and spiritual condition in which he finds himself. He raises the question because he cannot remain silent, and so seeks to secure release from his terrible inner tension.

That is why this manifestation is terrifying — because the LORD in wrath has arrived to take vengeance. Two terms represent Yahweh's wrath: *'aph,* "anger," "passion," "wrath"; *'ebrah,* the shape that wrath takes, "fury," "rage," "paroxysm," "craving for revenge." The verb *harah* (which RSV translates as a noun, "wrath") refers to fire that both blazes up and devours everything. These impulses to annihilation justify the approaching judgment and proclaim its near materialization.

Shortly it will become manifest that the object of the wrath which destroys is neither the rivers nor the sea, but the "puffed up" Great Power, Babylonia. However much it acted as "punisher," with the sin of presumption and pitilessness, it will not remain without being punished.

The text of v. 9a is very broken. It pictures the Commander-in-Chief equipped for battle in a cosmic setting, using the solemn expression of an oath of vengeance. [The RSV mg declares "Heb obscure."]

"Thy bow is stripped bare" (i.e., its covering cloth laid aside?), *'eryah te'or qashteka* (see the footnotes in *BHS*), describes Yahweh's positioning of his troops. This anthropomorphic picture signifies that the arrows are actually out of their quiver, the string is ready in his hand, and a shower of arrows floods over everything.

The significance of the word *matteh* is problematical. It means "shooting," "a shoot" or "branch" of a tree, "a twig," "an arrow," a "stick," "a marshal's baton," "an instrument of discipline," "a tribe," "a nationality." Among these various meanings, which should we take to help us since the sense of the word is so variable? The footnotes in *BHK* draw attention to a suggested alteration in the text: "Thou hast filled up the quiver with arrows" *(sibba'ta mattot 'ashpateka)* — the previous sentence leading by use of a synonym to the same thought. But this sentence could also be understood to show that Yahweh's promise (2:1-4) is now coming true, the promise he gave to the "tribe," the chosen people. *Shebu'ot mattot* could mean either "the arrows" of the oath or the oath "made to the tribe." Thus the word *'omer* in this connection means that the promise was becoming fact, was now being fulfilled. Yahweh's oath had two objects: the "puffed up" are receiving the punishment they deserve, while the "righteous" through faith shall live (see 2:4).

Verses 9b-12 picture the LORD's theophany in terms of a whirling tornado. We find analogous features in the book of Psalms

(18:8-16; 77:17-20; 89:10; 104:3-10). Thunder rolls in the whirlwind, lightning flashes in terrible darkness, the springs of the
deep burst up, the bottom of the seas becomes visible, the foundations of the earth reveal themselves. He uses the clouds as his
chariot and rides on the wings of the wind. The prophet experiences the noise of the frightful hurricane at Yahweh's riding
(rakab) and at the procession of vehicles of war. *Merkabah yeshu'ah*
offers an anthropomorphic picture to represent not merely chariots of war but Yahweh's victorious means of bringing liberation
and salvation to his people.

In the rendering of this theophany the prophet once again
turns to material from Israel's ancient tradition. He revives elements of the creation myth and bears witness to how in his work
as Creator Yahweh had revealed his might (cf. Ps. 33:6, 7; Job
7:12; 9:13; 26:10; 38:8); he cites the marvelous events at the Exodus, seeing them as decisive moments in the story of salvation
(Exod. 14–15; Judg. 5; Deut. 32–33; Isa. 51:9-15; 43:1-5, 15-21;
41:18; Ps. 77:17-20; 114 in parts).

In Israel's world of faith, knowledge of God as Liberator preceded knowledge of him as Creator. The Exodus had been the
decisive event in salvation history, and it was the Exodus that
had laid the foundations for faith in creation. Israel's Savior was
the same as he who had created the universe and brought into
being all life within it. In Habakkuk's prayer traits of God as
Savior and as Creator occur side by side. Habakkuk's witness
precedes that of Deutero-Isaiah and the exiled congregation. In
their faith, there is not simply a strong emphasis upon Yahweh's
double work—these are actually woven together and identified
in his person.

In this picture of the terrifying storm, the theophany grows
into a hurricane and swells into a deluge: "The earth poured forth
rivers," the result being that "the flood smashed the dike and
raised its hands on high" (vv. 9b, 10b). The verb *baqa'* describes
the cleaving of the earth, over which the waters of the earth's
deeps break forth, and the rain *(zerem)* pours down from on high.
Like a mighty wall of water it smashes through all embankments
and floods over the dry land. This description reveals elements
related to the representation of the Flood in the Priestly writings.
There the springs of the deep burst up with "crushing force" over
the *raqia'*, and the mighty wall of water *(mabbul)* surges over the
ground and submerges it (Gen. 7:6, 12; 8:2; cf. Nah. 1:4; Ps. 46:4;
48:8). At creation Yahweh had set bounds to the mighty floods
(Gen. 1:6, 9, 10; Job 38:8-11; Ps. 104:9); now he breaks up their

banks and gives them free rein to flood the earth. The roar of the "primal ocean," *tehom,* enhances the terror of the situation; it "gives forth its voice," *natan qolo;* and the waves of the swollen rivers, plunging into the abyss, rise to the heights and are ready to sweep everything away.

Darkness enveloping the whole world enhances the description of this chaotic situation, because "the sun and the moon stood still in their place" (RSV "habitation"). The term *zebul* is an astral-mythological idea, referring to their heavenly "house," to which the sun "returns" in the evening, or where the moon "has its habitation," since it does not appear until evening in the ethereal sphere. So dreadful is this situation that even the mighty heavenly bodies cannot endure it; they seek protection in retreat, because Yahweh's flashing arrows *(hets)* and glittering spear *(henit)* have terrified them in his blinding stream of light. The mountains grow benumbed in convulsions as at the moment when a pregnant woman is in unspeakable pain (v. 10), for they behold that terrible LORD who "bestrides the earth in fury" and "tramples the nations in anger" (v. 12).

In the general picture of the theophany those traits revealing Habakkuk's God that defined the witness of the dialogue in chs. 1 and 2 are repeated here. Yahweh, Creator and Savior, is the mighty LORD of history.

The preceding description has served as a preparation for a proclamation on the decisive action that appears in vv. 13-15. The circle has gradually narrowed, and now Yahweh stands face to face with his true enemy, the "puffed up" Great Power. This confrontation and the resulting duel in the prophet's eyes was Yahweh's "marching forth" *(yatsa')* for the salvation *(yesha')* of his people *('am)* and of his anointed *(mashiah)* (v. 13). The prophet refers once again here to the events of salvation history. Throughout the story of his people Yahweh had always stood ready to intervene in events that threatened destruction, and he had always brought Israel forth victoriously from their time of trial. In witness to this, elements of Nathan's prophecy to David came alive when he reported on the promise of an everlasting dynasty (2 Sam. 7:13-16; 23:2-5; cf. Ps. 18:51; 20:7; 28:8; 132:17-18). The word "anointed" has a collective significance; it does not indicate either the contemporary king or the high priest but refers to the chosen people (Isa. 61:6; Ps. 28:8; 84:10; 105:15).

The victory over the "wicked" is described in a twofold picture. "Thou didst crush the crown, the pate, from the house of the godless, uncovering its foundations up to the neck" (v. 13). The "house" means the Babylonian royal palace, and it symbolizes the royal rule. The picture stands connected to the preceding manifestation of the storm. The glittering spear was a powerful symbol of this, as it reached the royal residence with such a thrust that, beginning from the pinnacle, it pierced right through to its foundations, dug deep in the earth *(mhts)*. Under the weight of the blow the royal palace was smashed to pieces, reduced to rubble. Its base, which ensured the house's stability, was laid bare "up to the neck," that is, such a deep fissure appeared that only its neck was visible. What the image was seeking to express was that the palace was split to its foundations and so was turned into a ruin.

The material in vv. 14a and 15 completes the picture. As it seeks to flee out of the ruins the Great Power finds itself face to face with the LORD, its duellist; with his own sword he pierces the head of the military commanders. Again we find dependence upon the Song of Deborah (Judg. 5:26), where Jael pierced Sisera's temple with a tent peg. Here then is the ultimate completion of that fate about which the prophet had received a promise in his vision (2:1-5).

Verse 14b is a "bill of indictment" that unifies and summarizes the deeds of the oppressive, tormenting Great Power (1:13, 14, 17; 2:8, 10, 16). It carries forward directly the events that follow as a result of the whole collapse (586 B.C.), that is, when Jerusalem is to become a ruin, the temple is to be plundered, and everywhere blighted walls will tell of the havoc caused by Nebuchadnezzar. Yet, despite the fall of Jerusalem, Yahweh's promise will still stand. Desolation may indeed ensue, but the chosen people will not disappear, despite the Babylonian Exile.

The vision characterized by elements of the Exodus tradition closes with: "Thou didst trample the sea with thy horses, the surging of the mighty waters" (v. 15; cf. Exod. 14 – 15). Just as once Pharaoh's horses and chariots had perished in the waves of the Red Sea (Exod. 15:4), so too this will happen to the tyrannical Great Power: by the decree of Yahweh it will disappear without a trace.

The Prophet's Response: Horror, Joy, Trust (3:16, 18-19, [17])

Habakkuk's theophany with its excruciating experience ends (v. 16) with an expression of joy that comes about through liberation; we meet with a trustful hope for the future painted once again in a colorful picture.

Verse 16 is about the prophet's experience as he reacts to the theophany. Physical symptoms accompany his inner experience: trembling body, chattering teeth, bones shaking, feet tottering. This is the kind of reaction that reveals he has truly comprehended and accepted the meaning of his prophetic experience. It shows that, so far as human beings are concerned, the *dabar*, the "Word," is always a foreign force, one which a person such as a prophet can respond to only with great inner shock. On hearing of Yahweh's deeds that he had performed in the past, the prophet was aghast, for he felt the judgment was also about future events. Other prophets went through a similar experience at the time of their call (Isa. 6; Jer. 1; Ezek. 2 – 3), or when in a dream they heard the explanation of the divine disclosure (Dan. 7:28; 8:18, 27; 10:8, 16).

The appearance of Yahweh as army commander and the contemplation of his victory not only fill the prophet with fear but also arm him with trust for "the day of trouble" *(yom tsarah)*. This "emergency situation," strictly speaking, is what the "puffed up" avoids, the "narrow corner" *(tsrr,* v. 13b) where his fate is sealed. The prophet's faith enshrines endurance, steadfastness, and obedience, ensuring tranquility for himself *('anuah),* that kind of peace of mind whose source is the awareness of Yahweh's protection and trust. The verb *gwd* ("come between, intervene") indicates that the prophet becomes aware of the development of two opposite poles of lifestyle: while the enemy is in a "narrow corner," from which all possibility of rescue is excluded, where he will remain till the time of punishment, the prophet will live secure in undisturbed peace. True, the prophet does not concretize such a lifestyle in an historical situation, yet in it he hints at hope for a way of behaving in days to come when the catastrophe of 586 meets up with them, despite the successes of the Babylonians, for these will only mean the digging of their own grave. Such is the prophetic sight of him who stands on his watchtower, the vision of a prophet who hearkens to his Lord.

The intrusion of v. 17 breaks the report of his experience and of his expression of confidence for the future. It brings into view a critical moment in the future arising from a series of natural disasters. It speaks of famine and want such as endanger man's earthly existence. This verse counts on the later observations of an unknown editor, with a probable explanation of the *yom tsarah,* or with a nearer definition of it. This insertion can be attributed to that editor who finalized the order of thought when the theophany was turned into a liturgy and found its place in the congregation's "Psalms of praise." Its purpose, to which the exigencies of the situation give suitable reference concerning the prophet's judgment on the situation, was to hint at natural disasters that covered both the plant and the animal world.

This witness was further emphasized when the unknown author drew attention to the prophet's awareness that Yahweh was not only the Director of the fate of the nations and Savior of the peoples throughout history, he was also, as Creator, Ruler over his creation, so that in his judgment upon humanity even the flora and fauna shared. A double judgment is the issue here—a perceptible non-productivity in the plant world and the decimation of the animals. *Prh* means "to sprout," "to produce," "to be verdant," "to flower," "to produce a fruitful branch." A barren fig tree is being described. It has got into such a state that it cannot promise any fruit, and so its harvest fails. *Yebul* is produce, fruit. There is no fruit on the vine either. The produce of the olive tree *khsh*, "tells a lie," it fails (RSV). The fields do not "make" food, they do not give any produce. People are not guaranteed provisions, and so there follow want and misery. The flock is cut off from the stable, the ox from the farmyard. This is a description of a disease that has spread throughout the domestic animals, so that the stock of animals has dropped away.

Verses 18-19 contain proof of the prophet's strength, born of the liberating faith that produced it, and which gave him both joy and confidence as he looked to the future.

In his narration the prophet gives an account of real data, as instruments of Yahweh's judgment. No matter if the coming catastrophe be unstoppable, and if he cannot extricate himself from under its weight—he waits in inner confidence and rejoices in the God of his salvation. That is how he can begin his prayer with the introductory word "Though," "Yet, despite everything." This is the prophet's triumphant avowal, that he recognizes that the Lord who is coming to deliver his people is the same saving God whom he experiences in his own personal life! (cf. v. 13a). The human response to the experience of this deliverance and preservation is joy, an exultation overflowing out of the human heart (*'lz* and *gyl*).

It is not a question here of something casual or of mere human cheerfulness or enthusiasm, but of a deep calm arising from an inner harmony placed there by Yahweh. It gushes up from the heart and in consequence sounds from the lips as a burning witness. This inner transformation of a person resulting from an act of Yahweh the prophet describes in the language of the Psalms: "The LORD God is my strong refuge *[hayil]*; he has made my feet like hinds' feet" (Ps. 18:34; 2 Sam. 22:34; Cant. 2:8). The picture represents the lighthearted and secure gait of the deer as it bounds over the hills without ever stumbling. It is a description of the person of faith in the sense of *'emunah*, one who has received strength and resolution, who is no longer fettered by temptation, who is no more oppressed with the weight of doubt. Yahweh's strength has brought him release. Consequently he can stand still when under affliction and walk with confidence in times of oppression. His exultation is in the strength of the LORD and his walk is upon "the heights," again in the language of the Psalms (9:2; 13:5-6; 18:33; 28:7; 35:9; 68:4). This same picture comes alive in the Blessing of Moses (Deut. 33:29). The picture and expression is connected with Yahweh's triumphant "march"; in his steps there follow salvation and the preservation of mankind. This "freedom of the mountaintops" opens up a wide horizon with a broad view and offers a sure means of finding one's bearings in life.

The prophet's vision ends with musical directions. The theophany has been formulated in the shape of a prayer. *Neginotay* means an accompaniment by stringed instruments, perhaps a flute or a harp, such as was frequently the case in the public worship of God.

THEOLOGY OF THE COMING DAY OF WRATH

A Commentary on the Book of
Zephaniah

The great day of the Lord is near. . . .
A day of wrath is that day.
                                    —Zephaniah 1:14-15

CONTENTS

INTRODUCTION

ZEPHANIAH'S PERIOD AND PERSON

The heading of the prophecy (1:1) places Zephaniah's service in the days of King Josiah (639-609). Details from within the text of the prophecy confirm this period and define it more exactly.

Verse 4 of ch. 1 points to the exercise of a syncretistic religion in that period. In the prophet's time, both in Judah and in Jerusalem, people knew and practiced the Canaanite cult of Baal, Assyria's religion of astral mythology (or star worship), and the cult of the god Moloch, which originated among the Ammonites. Our prophetic critique, aimed at those cults that were undermining the pure monotheism of the worship of Yahweh, leads to the conclusion that Josiah's reform of the cultus had not yet taken place. We are thus at a period preceding the Deuteronomic reform of 622 B.C.

Verse 8 of ch. 1 highlights Zephaniah's castigation of the "officials" and of the "king's sons." This reference suggests that Josiah was still a lad, for there was a regency in Judah in the period when the prophet was active (2 Kgs. 21:1).

The prophecy against Assyria (2:13-15) infers that this great power is at the peak of its glory: "I am and there is none else." Its capital city, Nineveh, is specially mentioned (2:13), along with its palaces and its gardens; these all emphasize that Nineveh was the cultural center of the "far east." This observation leads us to conclude further that we are at a date well before 612, since the fall of Nineveh has not yet taken place.

From these reference points we are led to conclude finally that Zephaniah must have made his appearance after the period of the dark reigns of Manasseh (687-642) and of Amon (642-640; see 2 Kgs. 21 and 2 Chron. 33). After almost half a century of prophetic silence, among a group of new witnesses we find Zephaniah in the last decades of the 7th century alongside the prophets Nahum, Jeremiah, and Habakkuk. According to this reckoning he came to the fore ca. 630, in the first half of Josiah's reign in Judah, and served primarily in Jerusalem.

The above data, which follow from the total witness of the prophecy and can be substantiated from history, completely preclude the supposition of some scholars that the prophet must have served immediately before the Exile, in the period of Jehoiakim and Zedekiah (608-587).

With regard to the prophet's own person the heading supplies us only with his name and with his family line going back over four generations.

His name *Tsephanyah* means "the LORD has hidden," or "the LORD has caused to be hidden." This name was common in Israel (e.g., Jer. 29:29; 52:24; Zech. 6:10, 14); and while it bears witness to the might of Yahweh in general, it witnesses in particular to the power that preserved the prophet in the period of Manasseh's cruel reign (2 Kgs. 21:16).

The author's intention in tracing the prophet's family three generations beyond his father remains a mystery. Such a reference is quite surprising; it is in fact unique among the headings of the prophetic books. Such editing could be merely awkward, but it could also be deliberately and purposefully done. It is probable that the editor wants to establish the fact that the prophet originates from the royal line and that he is of Judean origin; so he is witnessing to the fact that King Hezekiah was his great-grandfather. By doing so he was getting around the possible misunderstanding arising from the name of the prophet's father, Cushi; that name might suggest that he was of Ethiopian or Negro origin, and thus a foreigner (cf. the Introductions by Kaiser, Fohrer, Bentzen, Smend, Rendtorff). It is possible that originally he used only his father's name, but that the exilic editor, whose purpose was in conformity with the Deuteronomic law (Deut. 23:8ff.), added in the other three generations (Sellin). It is worth noting too that the name reveals neither a national nor a racial significance; for some reason, however, this name of bedouin Ethiopian origin was now applied to an Israelite (Rudolph; cf. Van der Woude). Whether this editing was done by chance or deliberately, one thing is sure: in his sovereign manner, God elects his prophet. One could speak of a royal prince as being God's instrument, yet the instrument could be equally a Negro slave (Elliger, Keller).

The circumstances of the prophet's life are completely unknown. So we have to gather our information independently of the prophecy.

We note how well the prophet knows the capital city and its leaders. He gives precise topographical descriptions of Jerusalem.

He refers to the royal palace (1:8-9), to the temple mount and its neighborhood (1:10-11), to the merchants who were located in the valley according to their various trade corporations (1:11), to the Old City (1:12-13), and to the New City (1:10-11). As well he is acquainted with the territories beyond Jerusalem and Judah: the seacoast occupied by the Philistines (2:4-5), the home of their fierce enemy; Assyria far to the north with the great buildings of its capital city, Nineveh (2:14); their eastern neighbors, Ammon and Moab (2:8-10); and Egypt to the south (2:12).

Zephaniah is a relentless critic of his age. He knows well the leading strata of society and castigates them severely: the royal court (1:8-9), the priesthood (1:4; 3:4), the judges and officials (3:3), the merchants and financiers (1:11), and the conceited rich living complacently in complete disregard of their fellows (1:12). More than all it is the cult and the priests who are in the forefront of his criticisms, but he does not avoid paying attention to the great social and moral offenses arising from the greed of those in authority and from their misuse of their official positions. All this defines the religious and moral life of the chosen people, and through their violation of the Law makes clear that they were breaking the Covenant.

Zephaniah is well acquainted with the works of his eighth-century predecessors. His preaching is rooted in the prophecies of Amos, Isaiah, and Micah. It could be argued, as Gerleman believes, that he was a later disciple of Isaiah, and that he belonged to that group in Jerusalem that withstood the cultic prophets, and from which the Deuteronomic reform originated. Behind the central theme of his prophecy, behind his annunciation of the *yom Yahweh*, the Day of the LORD, stands the prophetic tradition of Amos (Zeph. 1:7-13, 14-18; Amos 5:18-20). In like manner also we learn of his summons to seek the LORD (Zeph. 2:3; Amos 5:4, 6), and to uphold his *tsedaqah*, the LORD's rule of righteousness (Zeph. 2:3; 3:5; Amos 5:15, 24). The call to humility, ʿanawah, is a heritage from Isaiah, and as in the latter's case, holding to it was the only possibility (Zeph. 2:3), in terms of a faith that clung to Yahweh (Isa. 7:9; 30:15). The returning "remnant" "will no longer be haughty in my holy mountain" (Zeph. 3:11), but they will call upon the name of the LORD with one accord for help against the assembling peoples, and will serve him (3:8-13; Isa. 2:4ff.).

In Zephaniah's vocabulary we meet with many expressions that remind us of the rich store of words to be found in the Wisdom literature, such as: *musar*, "correction," an instrument in education (3:2, 7); *ner*, "lamp," an instrument for giving light; *dal*, "lowly," humiliated (3:12); *ᶜanawah*, *ᶜani'*, "submissiveness," "meekness" (2:3, 12); *barur*, "pure"; *baqash*, *darash*, "seek," search, inquire (1:6; 2:3); *tsedaqah*, justice corresponding to Yahweh's righteousness; *ᶜawlah*, deceit, treachery (3:5); *mirmah*, guile, fraud (1:9); *hamas*, violence, terror (1:9). His use of these expressions points to Zephaniah's contact with the royal court at Jerusalem where the "Wisdom school" was located, or even to his actually belonging to it.

In the light of the above information, we can conclude without doubt that Zephaniah was of Judean origin, that he mixed in leading circles, and that he served in the first half of the reign of Josiah.

THE BOOK OF THE PROPHET ZEPHANIAH

Zephaniah's book consists of three chapters. It reached its final form in the Exile after a lengthy development. At the beginning short, varied prophetic utterances, in the form of "word of mouth" tradition, remained alive where worship was carried on and in the teaching of the circle of disciples. At a later time these oracles were written down. When the prophecies were collected and began to be arranged in order, the editor systematically shaped the book into its present form in accordance with the characteristic threefold eschatological schema to be found in the books of the great writing prophets. This threefold editorial division reveals itself as follows:

1. Judgment on the Day of the LORD's Wrath, 1:2 – 2:3
2. Announcement of judgment upon foreign nations and upon Jerusalem, 2:4 – 3:8
3. Prophecies of universal salvation, 3:9-20

To define exactly when each separate prophetic utterance or collection of utterances was made is not possible. Similarly, to define exactly the *ipsissima verba* of the prophet is not possible. Fohrer believes he can pinpoint them in those sections that deal with the pronouncement of judgment upon Judah and Jerusalem (1:4-5, 7-9, 12-13, 14-16; 2:1-3), and upon Philistia (2:4); while the judgment on Assyria (2:13-14) he sees as probably Zephaniah's; finally he regards 3:6-8 as an expression of collective judgment.

Without doubt the book assumed its form in a productive developing sequence. The prophecies against Moab and Ammon (2:8-11) found their place in the predictions against foreign nations; then follow a fragmentary prophecy against Ethiopia (2:12), and some sentences put together in 3:1-13; finally, in several stages, prophecies on salvation in 3:14-20. These sections originate in the period after the Exile, their format having been influenced by Deutero-Isaiah. These announce universal judgment (cf. 1:2-3) and universal salvation (2:11; 3:9b-10). The latest sections are to be attributed to a period after the return from exile, and thus originate from the time of the restoration, the closing declaration being 3:16-20. Here there appear the typical eschatological motifs of the later period — the overcoming of the power of the enemy, the restoration, the gathering together of the diaspora, the promise of a safe and peaceful life, and the enhancement of the chosen people before the eyes of the pagans.

The condition of the text is generally speaking unimpaired. Yet there are problems of interpretation at 1:3b; 2:1, 12; 3:3, 18.

The NT cites the book of Zephaniah in four places: Matt. 13:41 (Zeph. 1:3); Rev. 6:17 (Zeph. 1:14); Rev. 14:5 (Zeph. 3:13); Rev. 16:1 (Zeph. 3:8). All these texts reveal an eschatological outlook and direct the congregation's attention to the last judgment. Thus when the NT refers to the basic theme of the book of Zephaniah, it gives foundation to the prophetic view of a coming general judgment.

THE THEOLOGY OF ZEPHANIAH

The central point of interest in Zephaniah's theology is his proclamation of the *yom Yahweh*, the Day of the LORD. This peculiar *theologoumenon* of his gathers up into focus the various strands of his message; across the prophetic tradition it becomes rooted in Israel's credo.

The seed of this proclamation is to be found in the faith of the chosen people. It belongs to their outlook in their particular "time" and their view of history. Yet it is difficult to reconstruct the form it took as it evolved, beginning as it did with the acts of Yahweh in the earliest period. In his acts as Israel's *moshia‘* (savior) and *bore’* (creator), he revealed himself both as his people's Deliverer and Creator and as their unconditionally powerful and sovereign LORD. Ever since the deliverance from Egypt this Yahweh had been the God who had fought for his people (Exod. 14:14; 15:1-23), ever helping them to be victorious. At the period of the conquest too Yahweh's victories were those that evidenced the sure fulfillment of his promises. Israel was always victorious in the sense that it shared in the victory of the LORD! (*nosha‘;* see Num. 10:9;

Deut. 33:29; 2 Sam. 22:4). These victories are clearly visible in the days of the Judges as the acts of the LORD. At Isa. 9:4, the phrase "the day of Midian" indicates that significant moment when, in God's presence, Gideon reaped a brilliant victory with a very reduced number in his army (cf. Judg. 7:22-25). Yahweh took upon himself the people's battles both at the conquest and in the period of the Judges. This war, as G. von Rad points out, possessed a sacred significance. There was no thought of the war as being one of merely conquering an enemy, but in every respect it was fought to guarantee the right of the chosen people to exist. It delineated the immutable decision of the Lord of the Covenant, which was that Israel must live with complete security upon that land which she had received as an inheritance by the decision of her God (*Der heilige Krieg im alten Israel* [Göttingen: Vandenhoeck & Ruprecht, 1951]).

Thus it was because of these people that Yahweh accomplished his victories, his "saving acts," that is, the *tsidqot Yahweh* (Judg. 5:11; 1 Sam. 12:7), or the triumphs of the LORD. These rendered possible — in fact guaranteed — Israel's existence and sharpened Israel's distinctive lifestyle.

The prophetic proclamation of the Word thus discovered the concept of the *yom Yahweh* as a reality of faith already there. In view of this, the period conveying Yahweh's acts stretched out toward the future. It embraced not only the past and the present, but united itself with the future as the time when still more acts of the LORD would be realized. Israel always knew that its life was in the hand of God, whose might was directed to the issue of calling mankind to account, to the execution of justice; this involved the proclamation of judgment and of mercy toward Israel and every nation upon earth. The *yom Yahweh* does not express the whole prophetic eschatology — just one aspect of it. Typical motifs of it are natural catastrophes, cosmic horrors, Israel's settling its accounts with its enemies, and the judgment of the peoples.

Up to the period of the "writing prophets" the Day of the LORD had a clearly positive content. With Yahweh's victories it announced the chosen people's liberation and sustenance, together with the annihilation of their enemies. A drastic change followed when Amos delineated the Day in terrible colors and announced Israel's inescapable judgment (5:18-20). Likewise with the prophet Isaiah (2:12-21; 13:6-13; 34:1-8), who speaks of the LORD of hosts breaking in pieces the arrogant, self-sufficient, idolatrous people and wholly destroying them. These prophets now adopt the revolutionary view that Yahweh is no longer fighting for his people but against them.

"The day of the LORD is at hand" declares Zephaniah (1:7, 14), and by this pronounces the inevitable coming to pass of events that were now imminent. The introductory formulas "And it will come to pass on that day" and "it will come to pass at that time" are phrases that indicate that point in time in which these events will happen. Peculiar to himself the prophet emphasizes that these events will not happen in an impersonal manner, since Yahweh alone is the subject of them, the only author of every event.

Zephaniah found the concept of the *yom Yahweh* rooted in two different prophetic traditions, different from each other in form and development yet with one content: "Yahweh is known through his acts."

The first witness to this is found at 1:7-13, with a cultic coloring, to which the liturgical formula *has* (RSV "Be silent") points. It calls one's attention to the LORD's drawing near and warns the worshiping community to express humble allegiance. The Day's approach is predetermined in the words: "The day of the LORD's sacrifice," *yom zebah Yahweh*. A century earlier Isaiah had declared: "The LORD has a sacrifice in Bozrah, a great slaughter in the land of Edom" (34:6). This "sacrifice" referred to the destruction of Israel's enemies, when Yahweh would wage cosmic war, in which the hosts of heaven would take part (34:1ff.). In the same sense Jeremiah spoke of the judgment upon Egypt (46:27-28). Rooted in these prophecies, Zephaniah's witness, with a judgmental purport, completes them with what has not yet been experienced — Israel, the chosen people, is to be the sacrifice, and this all the nations of the earth will see.

The second witness is at 1:14-18, which reminds us of Amos's prophecy (5:18-20). This "day" will have a special sign — *gadol* (great). It will be *the LORD's* great day, so the sign of it ("great") will not be merely formal but will be evidenced in the signs contained in it. Yet there are formal elements, such as alliteration, whose timbre is in tune with its contents, enhancing the seriousness of the pericope, its oppressive sound, all emphasizing the approaching judgment. Five sonorous pairs of nouns illustrate the terrible nature of the Day's events.

Both sections of the text declare with a united intensity Yahweh's judgment, the deeds of the LORD, and in this way signal the range of events that will reach their conclusion at the cosmic level, condemning the covenant people and all the nations of the world alike. The events possess no human, historical, or political motivations whatsoever; the only subject is the LORD. Zephaniah's picture of the *yom Yahweh* is in fact a description of the LORD's actions. Therefore it is not a case of a statistical account; it is the portrayal of dynamic events. As a result it is in the depicting of these dynamic events that we find the prophet's "theology." It is an authentic picture of God that is trustworthy as a revelation of what humanity is really like, unveiled as in a mirror, so that humanity's social and ethical traits are clearly distinguished.

In Zephaniah's preaching Yahweh is the Creator of the universe, the Judge and Deliverer of his people, the God of the Covenant. On that day, the great Day of Wrath, this LORD will appear as witness (3:8, with the LXX); he will search Jerusalem with lamps (1:12); he will call his people to account (1:8, 9, 12); he will make an end of them (1:18); he will pass judgment on the pagan great powers (2:4-15) and on the officials of the covenant people (3:1-4). Anthropomorphic pictures acutely illustrate him as the LORD of judgment. He searches the holy city with lamps (1:12), accuses the nations on the basis of the incontrovertible nature of their deeds (3:8), and drives the people to panic (1:18). The verb *paqadti* ("I will punish") as a basic term occurs three times (1:8, 9, 12). The root *pqd* characterizes God as he who, on the basis of his proprietary rights, may call those of his "house" to account. The nuances in this illustrative process reveal at once the peculiar concerns of the Lord of the house. He had provided in his great goodness for the inhabitants of the house, had given them authority to see to its welfare, had arranged their various responsibilities, and now was calling them to give account. With his unexpected appearance he scrutinizes his home, estimates what is lacking, and passes judgment.

As the language of the OT developed, later on this term came to emphasize the end purpose (Gk. *episkeptomai*) of the thinking of the Lord of the house; in connection with his house he lays stress on his particular aim and emphasizes it. Without a doubt these features refer to the Lord of the Covenant who calls himself *'el poqed*, the God who visits, in the Decalogue, calling to account those who break the Covenant to the third or fourth generations (Exod. 20:5; 34:7; Num. 14:18; Deut. 5:9).

Yahweh's intervention shows up first of all the chosen people and its leaders: "Woe to her that is rebellious and defiled, the oppressing city" (3:1). This revelation leads in three directions: to God, to one's fellow human beings, and to where they meet in the cult. These three levels express the chosen people's basic interrelationships. The chosen people is rebellious, seditious, and recalcitrant, *mor'ah;* they do not listen to their God and do not accept his instructions, *musar*. The LORD of the Covenant had desired to formulate the covenant fellowship by means of these in accordance with his will. But missing here was any trust and any readiness to perform God's will. The word *nig'alah* ("defiled") refers to the uncleanness of the cult, to Jerusalem's befouled worship. According to the prophet's indictment — it is just here that the contrast shows itself — the holy city's vaunted cultic purity was only a show, because behind it there lurked serious sins. Those officials entrusted with the service presumed upon their positions of authority; they not only degraded their office, they completely profaned it (3:3-4). All of them — the prophets, the priests, the judges, and the authorities — had become faithless stewards and had betrayed Yahweh's concerns.

On the ethical level the all-embracing expression is *yonah,* "oppressing," doing violence, trampling down, robbing people of their rights. Clearly the prophet is referring to social abuses that he had actually experienced in his own circumstances. From out of such basic sins it was natural that there grew and flourished sins that affected society. Arising from alienation from Yahweh in the area of public worship there followed sins that necessarily defined people's ethical conduct and social relationships. Where the true knowledge of God is lacking then the worship of God becomes degenerate and the bounds of community life dissolve. This is truly a chain reaction!

Within this situation the LORD makes his appearance. He is now regarded as powerless, in the words of those who say in their hearts: "The LORD will not do good, nor will he do ill" (1:12). Not only does he show them up and accuse them on the basis of their undeniable activities, he acts! — "I will bring distress on men" (1:17). This pictorial mode of expression once again reflects how proud, conceited, self-confident man — all of a sudden finding himself in a tight spot, squeezed into a corner, panting for breath, becoming panic-stricken — moves like a blind man, unable to find the way out (1:17). In this situation their priceless lifeblood is poured out like dust, their "entrails" *(lehum)* like dung, like stinking excrement, sent flying in all directions. In just such pitiful caricaturing figures the prophet sketches the governing bodies, the rich upper classes, the merchants who relied upon their treasures and who would give all their silver and their gold if only they could wriggle out of this judgment.

On the Day of the LORD everyone will be defenseless and impotent, stripped of every human treasure, not able either to defend himself or to purchase his freedom with it. The judgment's initiative is God's "jealous love" *(qin'ah)*, because of which he can tolerate no rival beside himself. The *'el qanna'*, the jealous God, the God of the Covenant, exercises his right of possession in his judgments; he protects that which is his own.

On the "Day of the LORD" the judgment is completed as it goes beyond the area of the life of the chosen people. This is seen in the judgment upon the surrounding pagan peoples, among them Assyria, whose end is to be complete annihilation; the prophet reports the devastation of the whole country and of all its inhabitants (2:4-15). Thereupon Zephaniah depicts his God as he who condemns the whole created world to judgment. In this affirmation the prophecy's universality strikes us with such piercing vehemence as is to be found in similar terms only in the preaching of Deutero-Isaiah.

The judgment is standing at the threshold; it is "born" *(ledet hoq,* 2:2), so that it is not possible either to withhold its birth at the moment determined upon, or to hold back the approach of the Day of the LORD. What can one do? According to the prophet what must be done is the only thing possible under the circumstances. "What are you thinking about? Come to your senses, you insolent nation!" It is remarkable that in Zephaniah's case we do not meet with the summons to repent that is so characteristic of the prophets, as shown in their use of the verb *shub.* Instead he refers to a repentance, a "turning around," with a concrete content that has regard for the actual situation. For conceited, apathetic people, involved with foreign cults, he gives three suggestions as the only possibility for changing their behavior: "Seek the LORD, seek righteousness, seek humility" (2:3). Those who have abandoned Yahweh, thus losing all direction and making for the wrong goals *(hata'),* these must feverishly seek *(biqqesh)* God's will, return to the starting point, and rediscover their lost God. As for the pursuit of righteousness, this is to be understood in terms of the covenant decrees, as it is bound up with ethical behavior within the covenant relationship. Finally, the pursuit of humility means a recognition of Yahweh's power and a bowing down in reverence before his presence: "perhaps you may be hidden on the day of the wrath of the LORD." This word "perhaps" does not express any uncertainty, but points to the fact that the final outcome is in the hands of God and is of his sovereign grace!

The covenant people are in a hopeless situation, in that the prophetic summons is futile, for Israel is not capable of "seeking" the LORD!

In this situation there is but one certainty: "The LORD within her is righteous *[tsaddiq]* . . . every morning he shows forth his justice" (3:5). What a striking conclusion this is: her charismatic leaders are no longer in their positions, all government has virtually ceased, because the collapse of the people has brought nothing but hurt; yet despite everything Yahweh is present and is at work. In the holy city where there is only disloyalty, falsehood, and oppression, there God administers justice. Yahweh takes his people's cause in hand, just where the officials plunge into deadly danger the affairs committed to their charge.

At the end of his prophecy (3:9-20) Zephaniah turns in another direction, signaled by "Yea [*ki* — I declare that], *at that time.*" Once again it is only Yahweh's deeds he lists; these will mark a decisive change, first for Israel and then for the heathen nations. Along with universal judgment upon the whole world, Zephaniah proclaims universal salvation. The prophet's eschatology is contained in the sections 3:9-13 and 3:14-20. Here he witnesses to the period of salvation in which the fate of the chosen people will be radically altered following upon the re-creative work of the LORD. Within this total transformation we meet with a significant concept in the prophet's theology, namely, the "remnant": *she'erit bet yehudah,* "the remnant of the house of Judah" (2:7); *she'erit ʿammi,* "the remnant (those who are left) of my people" (2:9); *she'erit yisra'el,* "the remnant of Israel" (3:13); along with the verbal root *sh'r* that occurs here, *hish'arti,* "I will leave" (3:12). This name, "the Remnant," refers to the newly re-created people of the time of salvation. This people not only survives the judgment and comes through the ordeal of the Day of Wrath, by which the continued existence of the people in the physical sense is assured; but it also receives a new way of life as the outcome of Yahweh's new creative work and becomes the firstfruits of the future. They are to be the "remnant," the coming congregation that is to be a "chosen race, a royal priesthood, a holy nation, a people for his possession [1 Pet. 2:9, RSV mg] . . . that you may declare the wonderful deeds of him who called you out of darkness into his marvelous light."

Such is Zephaniah's penetrating prophecy of judgment and of compassion upon the whole world. It is a "theology" of the coming "Day of Wrath" (1:14-15).

71

COMMENTARY

THE HEADING (1:1)

The heading of the book of Zephaniah shows a relationship to that of Hosea (1:1), Micah (1:1), and Joel (1:1). This heading may be attributed to the work of the Deuteronomic editor. In it are to be found the three basic elements that are expressed as the substance of all prophecy: (1) the Word of the LORD, (2) the prophet appears as mediator, (3) in a particular historical situation.

The heading emphasizes that it is with the Word of Yahweh that we have to do. The Word, *dabar*, always "comes," "becomes," *hayah*, because word and act are simultaneous. It interprets an announcement and mediates events in history. The Word's event is effective, but it does not result from human initiative or co-operation. Behind the Word stands the living, active, mighty LORD, the real author of events.

Every prophecy points to how this active LORD, by the word of his messenger, steps into history and there accomplishes his work. Just because of this, the prophet, the "sent" one, the ordained and "sent forth" ambassador, can never be the subject of his own prophecy but only its mediator in the human scene. Since the prophecy sounds forth in the presence of human persons, in terms applicable to people of all ages, it never sounds forth on an empty and uninhabited stage. It is always living persons or a living community who are the recipients of the Word and always in a particular historical situation. The prophet is the mouthpiece of the eternal Word, but at the same time he is also the child of his time, living and serving in a concrete historical situation. The prophet unites the proclamation of the LORD who has called him with a living congregation in its particular historical situation, to whom he must faithfully transmit the message he has received. This double bond means that the prophet becomes rooted in his own period, yet, at the same time, he is witness to the formative deeds of the active LORD of history, bearing witness to these deeds unbendingly and fearlessly.

The Introduction above has dealt with the details of the heading.

JUDGMENT ON THE DAY OF THE LORD'S WRATH
(1:2 – 2:3)

This section is Zephaniah's lengthiest pericope. It consists of various types of prophetic material from various periods. We find in it threats, rebukes, and the pronouncing of judgment, and these follow one another in descriptive and hymnic forms. In form and content the various prophecies, only loosely connected with each other, are tied together by one basic idea — the Day of the Wrath of the LORD that is inevitably approaching, with judgment of total destruction upon the whole of the created world, including the chosen people. This pericope, constructed as a mosaic, reveals a kerygmatic and rhetorical unity (Rudolph). The editor's purpose ensures this by the creation of a redactional unity (Elliger).

Its basic theme is the announcing of the coming Day of Wrath, showing itself in two forms. The one has a cultic coloring in that it calls the coming time of judgment "the day of the LORD's sacrifice" (1:7-13). The other is a hymn painted in striking colors that lays bare the time of final devastation that is just ahead (1:14-18).

The original shape of this pericope may have been composed of 1:2-6, 8-13, and 14-17. To it v. 7 has been added in the course of editing; in content this verse resembles v. 14, but it has become wedged in between vv. 6 and 8. Verses 8, 10, and 12 have a similar introduction with their own coloring — "And on the day of the LORD's sacrifice — 'I will . . .' " (v. 8); "at that time I will . . ." (v. 12), in each case being followed by the word of the LORD, all of which is uttered in the first person. Verses 7 and 11 contain the reflection of the prophet, while vv. 13-16 give a description of the Day of the LORD now wholly in the third person. Verse 18 is the editor's own answer, and following the cry of 2:2 the pericope concludes by reiterating the universal judgment of annihilation. The whole section finds its conclusion in 2:1-3. It is rooted in the prophetic tradition (Amos 5:4-6, 14-15), and brings us to the realization of the possibility of an unavoidable judgment.

The text of 1:2 – 2:3 may be divided as follows:
1. Announcement of universal judgment, 1:2-3
2. Discrediting of Judah and Jerusalem, 1:4-6
3. Indictment of Jerusalem and its officials, 1:7-13
4. Calling to account on the Day of Wrath, 1:14-18
5. A hint of conversion, 2:1-3

Announcement of Universal Judgment (1:2-3)

These two verses are an overture to the pericope, announcing that the universal judgment is imminent. In form the speech is a prophetic threat. Judgment is coming upon the whole created world. The word *kol* points to this. It means every, all, whole, totality. In the OT this expression is used of the "whole" cosmos: the heavens, the earth, and all that is in them (Gen. 2:1 and 1:20-28). The Creator God reveals himself here, standing forth as judge, bringing a charge, and pronouncing sentence as in the days of the Flood (Gen. 6:7, 13). The one and only subject of these events is Yahweh, who has come to settle accounts.

The concept of annihilation, of a sentence that sweeps everything away, is expressed by the verbs *'asaph* and *suph* (v. 2). These two verbs complete and strengthen each other. *'Asaph*, as an infinitive absolute, means "gather together," "sweep up," "bundle together," as in gathering in the crops or collecting the troops together and stationing them for battle (Exod. 23:10; Lev. 23:39; 1 Sam. 14:52; Job 39:12). *Suph*, in the Hiphil imperfect, signifies "annihilate," "bring to an end," "fall into ruin," "cease to exist." The two verbs in such intensive association express the idea of total destruction. These agricultural and military expressions, taken from ordinary life, illustrate graphically how no one and no thing can extricate himself from Yahweh's sentence of judgment. The final destruction is not a form of fate, but the decree of the only Subject, God. The word *kol*, "everything," points to universal judgment, while the verbs *'asaph* and *suph*, "sweep away," represent the total annihilation. The expression *ne'um Yahweh*, "says the LORD," points to the finality of the divine decree, which is irreversible and valid over everything.

In v. 3 the decree points to the order in which it will reach completion—it will reverse the order of creation! (Gen. 1:20-28, P; Hos. 4:3; Ps. 8:9). It will light upon humanity in the first place, then upon the four-footed animals that live on the dry ground, then on the birds of the heavens, and finally on the fish of the sea. "Man," *'adam*, meets with a double reference, since "man made in the image of God" has a distinctive place in the created world with special responsibility arising therefrom. Seen from the way the verses are related to each other, man is responsible for the ruin that has come upon the created world, occasioning God's charge against him and consequent judgment. The prophet's universal outlook with respect to judgment appears here for the first time in the prophecy. This verse is the characteristic locus of Zephaniah's witness about God. Yahweh has not only elected his people and become the God of the Covenant, but also as its rightful Creator he is Lord of all creation and the prosecuting Judge of all peoples. What is lacking is a precise statement about the commencement of the devastation. The disclosure in the following lines is that Judah's and Jerusalem's sins at that time were evidenced in their breaking the Covenant, naturally drawing down upon them the judgment of God.

The fulfillment of the judgment becomes apparent in the expression *wehammakshelot ʾet-haresha ʿim,* which produces problems of interpretation.

Rudolph (p. 265) strikes the expression from the text as a foreign body that does not fit with what precedes it. RSV suggests "I will overthrow the wicked," omitting the phrase "I will put stumbling blocks" (see RSV mg). Under the influence of the LXX Sellin puts *basileis,* "kings," in parallel with *ʾadam,* "mankind," thus paralleling a people and its rulers. As many interpreters, so many suggestions.

Though problematic, however, the expression *makshelah* is very suggestive. The verbal root is *kashal,* with the meaning of "stumble" owing to not being able to see, and so to totter, slip, grope (in the Qal); to trip up, lead into sin, overthrow, make to stumble (in the Hiphil). The noun deriving from it, *makshol* (fem. *makshelah*), means an encounter because of which a person stumbles and falls into sin, the danger from the fall being hidden from him.

We must interpret this couplet critically in the light of the cultural setting of the prophet in conjunction with the contemporary religious and moral collapse. The prophet emphasizes that in this universal and sweeping judgment God will destroy those things which lead to sin and which predisposed the covenant people's depravity. It is clear that in the prophet's period these things were linked with those foreign cultic practices, whether of a material or of a spiritual nature, that were instrumental in bringing about Judah's fall. *Rashaʿ,* the wicked (v. 3b), may refer to the representatives of the foreign cult and to Israel's officials who had dissociated themselves from Yahweh and had caused the people to do the same.

Discrediting of Judah and Jerusalem (1:4-6)

Neither Judah nor Jerusalem can withdraw itself from such a world-encompassing and wholly sweeping judgment. Yahweh has narrowed down the circle and so has judged the chosen people. This section is an address of a prophetic and threatening nature in which the listing of contemporary, concrete sins gives reasons for the inevitable judgment. It makes mention of the political structure both of Judah and, separately, of Jerusalem with its traditional Davidic empire.

"I will stretch out my hand" (v. 4). This anthropomorphism is a pictorial expression describing the LORD as he prepares to execute his judgment. This same hand which so often had brought liberation and protection to the people (Exod. 6:16; Deut. 4:34; etc.) was now about to act in judgment (Exod. 15:12; Isa. 5:25; 14:26; 23:11; Jer. 21:5). The God who had shown himself in the eyes of Zephaniah's contemporaries to be impotent now is proclaimed by the prophet to be wholly capable of powerful action. The content of the picture in which the people had buried themselves was that Yahweh would never look on helplessly at the destruction of his people, since he had the power to intervene. The verb *karat*, "cut off" in RSV, means hew down, exterminate, lay waste, annihilate, erase. The expression exemplifies the seriousness of the sentencing, for it means complete extirpation. It refers back to vv. 2-3, to the universal judgment which will come upon the whole created world and from which the chosen people cannot expect to extricate themselves.

In expressing this decree of extermination God enumerates their actual sins. It is these that give the reasons for his wrath and judgment. Yahweh's judgment is always justified; he never acts from hearsay or impulse. The disclosure shows that everything is open to God's sight and nothing can be hidden.

The disclosure is made upon the basis of the "document" of the Covenant, the first table of the Decalogue, that is, on the first, second, and third commandments. These show that it is in fact the Covenant that has been broken. Yahweh brings to his people's notice four serious sins:

(1) *Baal worship*, the Canaanite religion focusing on fertility, especially that of vegetation, had been an unceasing temptation ever since the settlement in the land of Canaan. The prophet Elijah had contested the person of Baal and his ability to act before the eyes of his contemporaries. This was the great theme of the judgment at Mt. Carmel (1 Kgs. 18:21-46). The prophet Hosea again had protested against the fact that Yahwism was succumbing before this foreign cult. The same situation prevailed in Zephaniah's day when a syncretistic religion of a peculiar, hodgepodge nature was taking shape. "This place" (v. 4b) means before all else the holy place in Jerusalem, where every brand of Baal worship was being carried on. Presumably within those forms of worship the leaders had sought to honor Yahweh, but

thereby had blurred his monotheistic nature in the eyes of the
worshiping community. For this collapse those leaders of the cult
were responsible, whom Yahweh was now calling to account.

The RSV reads: "the name of the idolatrous priests" (Heb.
komer), and adds in a footnote, from the Hebrew, "with priests."
The word *komer* signified the priest of an idolatrous cult, while
kohen was a priest of the Jerusalem cult. Cutting off "the name"
of the leaders of that worship meant cutting off their persons and
dissolving their service, and at the same time wiping out all mem-
ory of their cultic community. The phrase "the remnant of Baal"
could not have been aimed at Josiah's reform of the cult, for this
idolatrous cult had been completely extirpated. We are dealing
with events before 622. This reference is much more likely to the
belief that in the end God will destroy Baal worship in all its
forms.

Verses 5-6 list the other three sins that were chiefly apparent
in the Jerusalem cult and among the capital city's inhabitants:

(2) In the period of Manasseh and of Amon *an astrological
mythological cult* originating in Assyria had found a home in Judah.
Because Israel was bound to Assyria in a vassal relationship this
cult had actually penetrated the holy place. The reference to
"those who bow down on the roofs" (v. 5a) is to the practice of
this cult, that is, people worshiping under the open sky. After
almost half a century of silence, when no prophetic word in that
dark period was to be heard, the voice of Zephaniah was among
the first to sound as he denounced idolatry in all its glaring forms.
So here it is not just Yahweh worship in a distorted form that is
in question; rather it is the denial of his monotheistic nature and
of his unique almightiness. The verb *shahah*, to bow down, render
obeisance, is an expression for praying. Thus it is no less than
a rebuttal of the first and second commandments. The verb *nishbaʿ*
(Niphal of *shbʿ*) means to swear as a religious action that is both
a profession of faith and an act of witness at the same time. In
the eyes of the prophet it revealed the irreconcilable difference
from the command: "You shall not make mention of the name of
any other god beside the name of God" (cf. Exod. 20:7), since
such a god does not exist and is only the offspring of your imagination! Throughout the prophet's words the God of the Decalogue protests against any affront to his autonomy. He is the God
who is the jealously loving LORD, who will not share his divine
nature with any other god.

(3) *Swearing by the god Milcom* (or *Malkam* in Hebrew) and the
offering of worship by his followers points to the adoption and

subsequent practice of this Ammonite cult (1 Kgs. 11:5, 33; 2 Kgs. 23:13). This divinity's name, from the root *mlk,* meaning "king," came to be pronounced with the vowels of *boshet* (shame, disgrace) — *melek* — *molek* — *molok.* The prophet's use of such words led to the idea that those for whom Molok (or Molech, Moloch) was "king" brought shame and disgrace upon themselves, leading to their final degeneration. For the rest Molok was the Moabite god of fire, in the Moabite language *kamosh,* to whom it was the custom to offer human sacrifice. The phrase "to pass a son or daughter through the fire" refers to this custom (Lev. 18:21; 20:2-5; Deut. 12:31; 1 Kgs. 11:7; 2 Kgs. 3:27). They attributed a propitiatory and cleansing power to this sacrifice. To swear by Molok meant to bear witness to his divinity, a prohibition of which is contained in the third commandment.

(4) Verse 6 refers to a group who were quite unconcerned either to honor the name of Yahweh or to interest themselves in the prevalent syncretism or even to practice any of the foreign cults. These were *self-confessed "liberals"* who, in their own estimation, kept themselves from involvement in any religious worship, living a lifestyle that was quite self-sufficient. These sundered all connections with Yahweh, thereby recognizing no obligation to obey him or to walk in his footsteps, *hannesogim me'ahare Yahweh.* This abandonment of and independence from God is a profound expression for what the RSV renders "who do not seek the LORD or inquire of him." These were "deserters of Yahweh"; they had no desire to know his will; and so they asked no *torah* from him — the verb *darash* meaning here "seeking," and *biqqesh* meaning "meeting" with him in the place of worship. Idol worship can take the form of worldliness and neutrality. In disclosing and in enumerating sins we can observe an upward-curving graduation from a vulgar, primitive form taken by idol worship up to its refined and "intellectual" forms.

Judah and Jerusalem were a "culture-community." They were Yahweh's covenant people. The God of the Covenant, the Creator and Sustainer of the cosmos, calls them to account and puts them on trial on the basis of the revealed Law.

Indictment of Jerusalem and Its Officials (1:7-13)

This section is another prophetic threat. The Day of the LORD is at hand, the day when the LORD will bring his punishment to pass. The moment of judgment grows ever closer. After heralding the judgment first upon the whole world, then upon Judah and

Jerusalem, the prophet next declares that Israel's officials will share the fate of all those who are now accused.

Conceived in accordance with a liturgical formula, v. 7 is a prophetic speech (cf. Hab. 2:20; Zech. 2:17) that leads on into the period of the judgment to come. Offering a picture of a sacrifice prepared and waiting to be presented, the prophet speaks as if it were his own affirmation. Once the sacrificial animal has been cut up and prepared for sacrifice, according to the cultic rules for a worshiping congregation, it is then "consecrated," made ready for reception at the sacrificial banquet. The priest was accustomed to announce the appearance of the LORD at the sacrificial banquet, declaring that he was actually taking part and was really present though invisible. So the congregation is called to silence — *has!* "Silence!", "Be quiet!" This was a sign for humble and respectful behavior on the part of the participants. The same expression occurs in pagan rituals announcing the presence of the divinity and reminding worshipers of the respect required before the *tremendum.* In connection with our text the *has!* is an intimation that silence must precede the arrival of the LORD, who is coming to act as Judge and is bringing his judgment to an irrevocable conclusion.

Zephaniah's announcement is rooted in the prophetic tradition. A century earlier Isaiah had proclaimed that "the LORD has a sacrifice in Bozrah, a great slaughter in the land of Edom" (Isa. 34:6), thus punishing the enemies of Yahweh's people. This battle assumes cosmic dimensions and involves the hosts of heaven (34:1ff.). In like manner Jeremiah, in connection with the judgment upon Egypt, heralds "the LORD's sacrifice" (Jer. 46:10) and Israel's liberation and preservation (46:27-28). In both instances the LORD's "day of sacrifice" is that point of time which will bring about the decisive event for the sake of the chosen people: Yahweh will render account with his enemies and Israel will be the invited guest to witness their destruction. Within this well-known prophetic tradition, Zephaniah completes a striking turnaround — it is the chosen people who are to be the sacrifice, and it is all the nations of the earth who are to be witnesses of the judgment!

Here again the only subject of events is Yahweh. He it is who prepares, *hekin* (Hiphil of *kwn*), the bloody banquet and consecrates, *hiqdish* (Hiphil of *qdsh*), that is, renders things suitable, for those taking part at the cultic banquet. In these two verbs the motifs of preparation and consecration are apparent. Only those who are cultically clean may participate at the sacrificial festival.

Consequently before they approach the sacrifice it is required that they complete the regulatory cleansing ceremonies, *hitqaddesh* (Hithpael of *qdsh;* Exod. 10:14; 19:15; Josh. 3:5; 7:13; 1 Sam. 16:5; 21:5). This means that God will equip the foreign nations to execute judgment upon the chosen people, arousing them against Israel just as the prophet Isaiah had declared: "I myself have commanded my consecrated ones, have summoned my mighty men to execute my anger" (Isa. 13:3). *Qeru'ayw* means guests, the enemy, the pagans, upon whom the sacrificial blood is intended to be poured out. It remains debatable whether the prophet's words could possibly have been intoned ca. 625 about the danger of an incursion of the west Asian Scythians, so that the reference was actually to the Scythians when the prophet spoke of "consecrated guests."

Verses 7-8 disclose what will happen on "the day of the LORD's sacrifice" at the time of judgment. The disclosure of this calling to account reaches to Judah and Jerusalem's executive stratum. *Sarim* is a collective term for leaders in the community. It can mean those invested with esteem in state positions, and so ministers, or the army officers who were responsible for state functions. *Bene hammelek* means "the king's sons." In this category we are to include princes of royal blood, those who advise in a period of regency, as when the young Josiah was first on the throne. The verb *paqad*, "punish," can mean look for, inspect, examine, discipline, punish, judge. This verbal root with its concentrated content describes God (1:8, 9, 12) as being responsibly committed to his property and so must bring it (i.e., Israel) to account on its home territory and pass sentence on it there. It has various shades of meaning. For example, it might describe a businessman who has liberally endowed his house with his goods and has then given authority to others to look after it, but at the same time has called them to be responsible for their faithless stewardship. Such features doubtless point to the Lord of the Covenant, who, in the Decalogue, calls himself *'el poqed*, the God who calls to account those who break the Covenant even to the third and fourth generation (Exod. 20:5; 37:7; Num. 14:18; Deut. 5:9).

The Prophet Lists Three Sins of the Leaders (a) *Arraying themselves in foreign attire* (v. 8). Wearing strange clothing was a mark of breaking with the traditions of the fathers. With it goes the taking over of a new lifestyle, new customs, new moral behavior. All this directly contradicts the prescriptions of a moral and religious faith in Yahweh. It was not only the Assyrian cult that had penetrated the holy place, but also its animating spirit. This resulted in a breakdown of faith among the covenant community. The prophet here is not just objecting to the inflow of strange fashions and the practice of them; rather he is looking to the root of the matter, for he sees here a clear sign of the parting of the ways from Yahweh. A person is subject to him whose clothes he wears. When Jonathan took off his robe and gave it to David (1 Sam. 18:1, 4), he was expressing the close relationship their friendship brought about. A person's inner being can be represented in some respects by what he wears, even though "clothes do not make the man." A change in the outward impression he gives can be motivated from a change within.

(b) *The officials who "leap over the threshold"* (v. 9a). This is a reference to an ancient Philistine superstition. The god Dagon had his seat at the threshold of the temple at Ashdod (1 Sam. 5:5). As a sign of respect, therefore, one had to jump over the entrance to avoid stepping on the god's head and thus bringing danger on oneself. It was the custom of the royal house of Persia to cross the threshold of the palace stepping with the right foot only. This was the way one expressed homage and respect for the court. The prophet here denounces taking over any such foreign concept.

(c) *"Who fill their master's house with violence and fraud"* (v. 9b). One can think of "their master's house," *bet ʾadonehem,* as the temple, decorated with all kinds of Assyrian paraphernalia, which the prophet branded as "violence," *hamas,* and "fraud," *mirmah.* But it would be more appropriate to understand *bet ʾadonehem* as "royal palace" or "royal house," where symbols of a corrupt spirit taken from paganism had invaded and destroyed the pure Yahweh cult. Zephaniah, as one who belonged to the royal house and who was well acquainted with its surroundings, does not mind naming all those perversions which he experiences in their social and ethical relationships. He condemns every influence, every abuse of power, fraud and deception based on all kinds of deliberate misrepresentation. The contemporary officials who had taken those strange customs into their inner being had gone through a great transformation and were displaying a spirit measurably different from Yahwism. They did not take alarm at the most debasing abuses, if only these accomplished their own desires. We can think here of the machinations of various kinds of faithless stewards, brutal in their oppression and misappropriation, even more so in the area of the spirit, their abuse of their official authority (3:3-4). The prophet here emphasizes the symptoms that point to defects of the heart and of the conscience—symptoms that speak of departure from the LORD and make a root apostasy apparent. These things are sure signs of a corruption of faith.

After this disclosure there follows an announcement of the judgment upon the governing circles (vv. 10-13). The prophet speaks in the name of the God who acts, who has begun his judgment. This coming judgment is made apparent through his serious and pregnant sentences.

He employs many nouns and verbal participles to express his message. The "consecrated guests" (v. 7), that is, the enemy that has been consecrated to accomplish the judgment, are here in the capital city and are going to fulfill their commission. The prophet does not name the enemy; instead he describes Jerusalem's reaction—weeping, wailing, a cry for help accompanying the events. The prophet knows the capital city well and can point exactly to its topography.

Verse 10 describes the events of "the day of the LORD's sacrifice." The events following upon the judgment are to begin in Jerusalem. Jerusalem's geographical position provides it with significant protection. On its east, south, and west sides a steep cliff guards it, ensuring a natural protection. Only its northern side, which links up with the Judean hill country along a gentle slope, indicates its "Achilles' heel," where the city was vulnerable. In his inaugural vision, when the prophet Jeremiah refers to "danger breaking in from the north," he is indicating this particular geographical site (Jer. 1:14). The words "a cry," "a wail," "a crash" are all synonyms that heighten and illustrate the perilously rapid spread of the danger.

At the Old City's northern extremity the Fish Gate opened westward toward the New City, at the point where the ancient city wall intersected the "second" city wall that went back to the time of Solomon. The Fish Gate is mentioned in 2 Chron. 33:14; Neh. 3:3; 12:9. Through it the road led by the shortest route to the seashore. It is probable that fishermen entered the city with their catches by this route and sold them here; from this then the name would derive. From here too the northern part of the capital heard the cry arising, a cry of catastrophe, *qol tse'aqah*, a cry calling for help in time of danger. It was in this very expression that the seriousness of the situation was revealed, a helplessness in tight circumstances, and utter dependence on the help of others. *Mishneh* (RSV "Second Quarter") was the part of the city that was spreading southward, the Lower Town or New Town. Here the prophetess Huldah dwelt, as we find in the Deuteronomic scroll of 2 Kgs. 22:14-20. In Nehemiah's time this suburb had its own "overseer" (Neh. 11:9). It was from that quarter that a wail would be heard, *yelalah*, the cry of suffering humanity, and *sheber*, that is, the sound of crashing, cracking, of the crackling of fire. It is evident that the reference is to the heaps of rubble in the Lower or New Town. It is probable that the prophet means us to understand by this not only the temple and the palace hill but also the hills round about the Lower Town, such as Bezetha and Gareb (Jer. 31:39). It was in this new quarter that the city's fashionable mansions were built.

According to v. 11 the cry of terror reached also the city's business quarter, the area where the tradesmen and merchants lived. The horrible sound of the cry *yelalah* meant lamentation and wailing aroused by their sense of helplessness. The *Makhtesh* (RSV "Mortar") took its name from a hollow area, a quarry cut out of a hillside. It was situated in the area between Acra and Bezetha on the west and the spring of Shiloah to the east. It was what Josephus called *he ton tyropoion pharag*, the valley of the cheese-makers and of the fullers. Here was to be found the contemporary money market, the place of the Exchange. *Katash* means "pound," "smash," "shatter." The prophet uses this expression deliberately to describe the judgment that awaits the merchants and the money-brokers. That will be their fate, like a mill that breaks up the rocks at the rock-face, or like a hard object in a mortar. *'Am kena'an* the RSV translates as "all who weigh out silver," since it does not refer to the Canaanite people or to the Phoenician merchants. It refers to the trading element of Jerusalem. *Netil* (RSV "weighs out") means to load up, to lay up, to debit. So it speaks of being fully stocked up. It points to the contemporary practice of the shopkeeper measuring out the silver, with which he is paying or with which he is being paid, with a counterweight. The prophet is denouncing the businessman's view of life, his feverish commercial excitement, for in this too Zephaniah sees a departure from the custom of the fathers. The questions of everyday life the prophet enlightens from the point of view of the "Yahweh faith."

Once again God appears in an anthropomorphic picture (v. 12). He is like the police making a quick raid, a razzia, performing a search of the house and in this way discovering the sinner. Eastern houses were by and large dark; the day's sunshine could not venture in. A lamp, *ner*, on the other hand, could shed light on the piles of rugs stowed in the corners of a room. In Christ's parable the lady of the house searched for her lost coin in this way (Luke 15:8). Nothing can be hidden from Yahweh, for before him everything lies open. He brings to light everything that is hidden, and this is what he does too with Jerusalem's sins. The verb *paqad* that occurred at vv. 8 and 9 means just that: as the owner he inspects everything, makes himself fully acquainted with the existing state of things, indicts the persons in question, and then pronounces the verdict. This verse makes plain the judgment upon the self-centered, self-satisfied, apathetic, uncultured citizenry who were living their lives with a false sense of security.

The prophet uses a suggestive picture to show up their lifestyle — they are "thickening upon their lees." *Qapha'* means to curdle, coagulate, congeal, become gelatinous. A noble wine, even as it ferments, rids itself of the dregs. These accumulate as the "lees." Consequently one must draw off the wine from its lees, and so separate the fermenting liquid from the sludge. What he means is that there is nothing pure in those self-satisfied burghers and holders of office, with their whole confidence in life in their worldly possessions. This is because they are always one with their sins, and do not seek for cleansing in fellowship with God. More accurately, this spiritual lifestyle is an expression of laziness and stubbornness. It was in such a bored and apathetic mood that they conceived their opinion: "The LORD will not do good, nor will he do ill." This conclusion casts doubt on Yahweh's creative power and degrades the living God to the level of the idols. These "look on" dispassionately as the world rolls by, but cannot interfere because they are incapable of action. In this way of thinking it is Yahweh who is the powerless one; yet there is no need to reach this conclusion, since it is really blind chance that directs a person's fate and regulates his whole life. As a result of God's doing neither good nor evil, he does nothing! Totally unconcerned, he can wash his hands of everything to do with mankind. The inhabitants of Jerusalem are about to experience the contrary to that false view "on that day," when totally unexpectedly this "powerless" LORD will appear and call everyone to account.

That mankind's work and toil will turn out to be without effect will be evident from this terrible judgment (v. 13). What is said here is in acute contrast to the preceding verse! Those who supposed that Yahweh is incapable of concluding an issue whether good or evil are going to experience that it is their own work that has no point and is just a waste of time. "Though they build houses, they shall not inhabit them; though they plant vineyards, they shall not drink wine from them." Houses and vineyards symbolize the good life to which one can proudly point, but now all at once these are to become rubbish. They will no longer be usable, nor will they even be there to be enjoyed! The judgment may refer not only to the destruction of worldly goods, however, but also to a feeling of exhaustion arising from the never-ending uselessness of possessing things; or again from the realization that others will enjoy the fruit of one's sweated toil, and not the one who labored to produce it.

Those who trusted in their material goods and put their hope in those possessions they had gained through their work are now going to experience sorrowfully that everything is suddenly going to become mere booty and loot. It is the sack of Jerusalem that is referred to here, as v. 10 has already indicated. The plundering enemy who is going to cause this immeasurable destruction, ravage the city and sack it, is unknown.

Calling to Account on the Day of Wrath (1:14-18)

The prophecy assumes a hymnic form in the pericope of vv. 14-18. It hymns the imminent Day of the LORD, the Day of Wrath. A theme typical of Zephaniah appears here, in that we are looking at the *ipsissima verba*, the actual words, of the prophet where the form of speech is one with the self-disclosure of Yahweh's decision. It typifies his announcement about the coming judgmental acts. The concept of the *yom Yahweh* is to be found in the preaching of other prophets too (Amos 5:18-20; Joel 1:15; 2:1; 4:14; Obad. 15; Isa. 13:6; Ezek. 7:7). But what is wholly peculiar to the prophet Zephaniah is that he calls this day "the Day of Wrath." It is the time of the LORD's theophany. Yahweh will appear and will execute his judgment. This judgment will smite the chosen people. It is they who will be the sacrifice performed before the eyes of the foreign nations (v. 7). According to the Vulgate translation, *dies irae, dies illa* marked the day about which Thomas Celanoi (1255) was inspired to write and which became the words of that well-known hymn: "That day of wrath, that dreadful day." The alliterations in the Latin, along with the timbre of the verse, help to emphasize its awful seriousness and distressful mood. The hymn's construction is a work of art as it heralds the imminent Day of the LORD (v. 14a). It then describes that day itself (vv. 14b-16a), the acts of the LORD on that day (vv. 16b-18a), and concludes with "the end" (v. 18b).

Verse 14a signals the approach of this dreadful day. It is near, *qarob;* in no way can it be held back: it is *maher me'od,* "hastening fast." The prophet's comment indicates that it will not be in the power of man either to determine the time of it or to avert it. It is already at hand, inescapably here, while man is helpless. *Haggadol* (the "great" day) signifies that this day surpasses everyone's comprehension. Events will follow such as one cannot possibly struggle against; they will transcend one's capacity and ability to comprehend. The "sound" of the day will be bitter, *mar*, that is, what will fill that period will be bitter. The prophet describes its awesome atmosphere by emphasizing how even a warrior, a "mighty man," a "hero," *gibbor*, will cry aloud and wail. If then the intrepid "hero" cries out in fear, what will ordinary, helpless, simple, weak persons do?

He paints this day in dismal colors (vv. 15-16). This illustrative writing points to the seriousness of the judgment. The LORD appears, the God of judgment. The Day of the LORD is painted with the colors of war and of tempest. *'Ebrah* is wrath, a bursting out in anger, flooding in rage in all directions. The picture portrays the destructive wrath of Yahweh. The four following nouns in pairs, sounding in accord by means of alliteration, illustrate the day and its events — *tsarah umitsuqah*, "anguish and affliction" (NEB). In their terror people cannot get breath, they clutch at their throats, fear robs them of their strength, they are overwhelmed by panic, there is only *sho'ah umesho'ah*, "destruction and devastation" (NEB). Incorporated in this picture is the devastation caused by a hurricane, the ravaging of a tornado, the evidence of total conflagration and havoc at the hands of a cruel enemy — material destruction, homes in ruins, human beings butchered. *Hoshek wa'aphelah*, "darkness and gloom," as if it had cosmic significance, a darkness quite other than the oncoming of night (Exod. 10:21-23). *'Anan wa'araphel*, "clouds and thick darkness," a condition where there is no sun, resulting not merely in danger to health but actually in rendering impossible any biological life. These are all consequences which everyone will experience and from whose influence no one will be able to extricate himself. Insensitive, self-sufficient, self-satisfied, apathetic types will be overcome by such manifest realities and be brought to their senses when even the faintest ray of hope is removed by the hopeless darkness of that night.

Verse 16 illustrates the Day of the LORD's Wrath from another point of view. The judgment arrives like enemy forces storming a city. This is what the *shophar uteru'ah*, the "war trumpet," refers to — the sound of alarm. Such a bugle-call announced the opening of a festival (Num. 29:1ff.); but it could also signal a war cry, in pointing to the presence of the LORD of battles, who pits his might against his enemies (Hos. 8:1; Amos 2:2). This meant that Yahweh was himself the enemy of his people! This verse reflects back to v. 7. It was God's will that his people should become the sacrifice; as "the consecrated officials," they themselves were to bear the judgment. *He'arim habbitsurot* means cities that had been strengthened. The *pinnot gebohot*, "lofty battlements," were the several strong bastions that were Judah's fortifications. Before God there are no strengthened, fortified cities, no ramparts at the top of a cliff that could give protection in the time of judgment. By his decree Yahweh has rendered every human being defenseless and impotent.

In v. 17 the prophet lists the actions God sees fit for these impotent persons and in this way concretizes the judgment. We find still another very expressive anthropomorphism used — *hatseroti la'adam*, "I will squeeze man into a tight corner" (the Hiphil of *tsarar* emphasizing the effortless action of the subject!); God compresses man's chest so that he can no longer breathe. This deadly danger is expressed in masterly terms — where there is no breath there is no life! In such a situation people revert to panic; they try to escape, but move like the blind who find themselves in a strange setting and cannot get their bearings. The verb *halak* means not only walking, traveling, but also gasping for breath, stumbling about, searching for a way out. But there is no way out; the road to safety is hidden. The previous verses had produced a record of sins that the prophet now compresses into a short sentence, *layahweh hata'u*, they had turned away from the LORD, (not, as RSV, "sinned" against the LORD); they had mistaken the goal. The seriousness of the judgment is reflected most truly not just in the picture of destruction but also in that of taking booty. Not only will material goods become doomed to destruction, but that which is the greatest value in the created world — man himself — will become like a stinking dump-heap. That which conveys life, blood, *dam*, will become at the time of the enemy's massacre as cheap as the dust of the ground that is trodden under foot. Humanity's noble, inner self, the individual, the "persona's" secret source, the epitome of every human value, *lehum*, the inner being, the entrails, the marrow, the sap of life, will flow forth like loathsome excrement. In this verse it is Yahweh himself who is speaking and who is conveying the judgment he intends to execute. This then is "the day of the LORD's sacrifice," the time of slaughter to which v. 7 has referred.

It is total destruction that is predicted in v. 18. It is not only the idolatrous common people, nor even the top-level leadership, the rich merchants, the self-satisfied and totally indifferent masses, who are under judgment—it is the whole world. This section of the verse bears witness to the destruction that preceded the Exile, and to the events that actually took place during the Exile and were inserted into the prophecy at a later date.

Etched in cheerless colors, we see the merchant and rich aristocrat under judgment; both are outlined as figures of caricature, as they seek to escape through payment of gold or silver. No chance of escape exists! Any material basis for maintaining security has completely disintegrated. Nothing that man considers to be of value is any longer able to shield him or buy deliverance for him!

It is Yahweh's jealous love that nourishes this judgment and motivates it (v. 18b). *Qin'ah* means the jealous love of the God of the Decalogue that cannot tolerate any rival to himself. The *'el qanna'*, the "jealous God," watches over his own and refuses to share them with other divinities! Because of his right of possession, the fulfillment of this concept meant that he must necessarily defend his own from actions that touch upon his "sensory nerve." Yahweh is "angry" and convicts simply because he does not permit the one who is exclusively his own by right of his creation and redemption to become the property of a strange god. At no price will Yahweh ever give up what is his own! Even in his judgment he exercises his right of ownership. He may destroy, but he has the power to re-create!

A Hint of Conversion (2:1-3)

Employing a philosophical style, the author has a prophetic hint in this pericope. Closely connected with what has preceded, where the prophet had pronounced the finality of the judgment on the Day of Wrath, this section sounded forth *'ulai*, "perhaps," "it could be that." The prophetic hope lights up the coming darkness of the judgment. This "perhaps" in no way diminishes the breadth of the judgment whose concrete form the previous verses have displayed. There is not a word here of any inconsistency in Yahweh, or of his unexpectedly turning away from his original decision. The prophet points to God's compassion in the power of which he may suspend the judgment he has announced or else retain it.

The chosen people must prepare themselves to look the judgment in the face; they must do his commands, while leaving the outcome of events to the LORD. Do, he says, what you see to be the good. What is necessary above all is to recognize the actual situation and take it to heart. But this one thing they must do, and it is the only possible thing if they are to continue in these critical times. The prophet emphasizes that the only possibility of staying the judgment rests with the sovereign will of God. Thus the "perhaps" does not apply to humanity, for it is God's "perhaps" alone.

This prophetic intimation is made up of three elements: (a) an urgent demand (v. 1), (b) the reason for the demand (v. 2), and (c) advice on turning it into action (v. 3).

The exact meaning of v. 1 is problematical. Various interpretations of it have been attempted, as each scholar has sought to shed light from various angles upon its highly concentrated contents. The verb *qashash* (RSV "come together," as in Exod. 5:7-12; Num. 5:32; 1 Kgs. 17:10) can mean in a moral or spiritual sense "pull oneself together," "return to one's senses," "recognizing who one is" and what one's relationship is to one's circumstances. The Hithpael form of the verb can mean assembling together, standing close alongside others, recovering one's senses, recognizing who one is. The LXX has *synachthete kai syndethete:* "Congregate together and unite with each other," and the Vulgate virtually the same: *conveniente congregamini.* The Talmud has "Assemble together and bring others in too" (*Baba Bathra* 60b).

In the second half of the verse the Niphal participle, *miksaph,* signifies the cultic community that is being addressed. The verbal root *kasaph* speaks of what is meaningless, pale, shy, yearning, pining, impelled by inner desire, broken in spirit, full of remorse and contrition. Here then arise difficulties in interpretation. From this root the word *keseph* (silver) derives. When in a business transaction it is time to pay, it was the custom to cut through a bar of silver. In so doing the silver became colorless, like the remainder of it that had now oxidized. This act of cutting is seen as being "cut up" in a spiritual sense, with reference to repentance and remorse. Rudolph refers it to the conscienceless community that does not feel "cut up" at all. The LXX has *to ethnos to apaideuton,* "uninstructed people"! The Vulgate has *gens non amabilis,* "unlovable nation," whom God does not yearn for, *gens quae amore Dei indigna est,* a people unworthy of the love of God. This translation brings out not so much the apathy of the people as how in their whole way of life they showed themselves unworthy of the love of God, by not yearning for the Law of God (cf. Ps. 84:3; 42:1; 119:20; Job 7:2; Isa. 26:9); they were a people that displayed a spiritual laziness.

This verse is to be understood in connection with the previous verses. The word *haggoy* (RSV "nation") does not refer to the pagan peoples but to all those on whom the prophet has pronounced judgment — the chosen people and its leaders, the priests, the court officials, the army officers, the merchants, the financiers, the aristocratic rich, the self-satisfied, the apathetic citizens of the capital city. So it is actually these people whom the prophet calls to repentance and whom he summons to convert.

The reason for this summons is given in v. 2. The judgment is still there "at hand," but it has not yet fallen. Before, *beterem*, the appointment of that time (RSV mg "before the decree is born") points to that decisive moment which could bring the change at the time of the approaching judgment. The accomplishment of the judgment is given us in a clear picture — *ledet hoq*, "the birth of the decree" (not RSV "before you are driven away"). The prophet points out that at that critical time, even before the realization and completion of God's decree, the people can profit by the chance to grasp the one and only possibility of the judgment's being held back; they must do what is said in v. 3. In pictorial terms the prophet emphasizes two "moments"; the judgment is coming surely and inescapably. The actual moment of birth and the time when it will be fulfilled cannot be asserted; one can only know that Yahweh has made clear his decree, which can be neither undone nor postponed nor prevented. Just as a whirlwind snatches up the featherweight chaff and whirls it away without trace, so will the storm of judgment sweep everyone away when that day "passes over," *'abar*. The words *haron* and *'aph-Yahweh* picture the heat of God's wrath. It will consume like a flame of fire. The twice-occurring particle *'alekem* reveals the direction of the judgment — actually *you* will be the target of the judgment; there is no way *you* can escape the judgment.

Verse 3 counsels them to seek for action! *Biqqesh* means seek, search, struggle for, enquire about, ask someone's advice, seek his will. The form of the verb here is an intensive (Piel) imperative, suggesting urgent search; it concentrates on the idea of hard activity where the subject strives feverishly for what has been lost or has disappeared, and will seek with all his might till he finds it. "With unwearying perseverance you must seek to reach your goal, until you find what you seek for." The prophet is here activating his apathetic and obstinate people. The same verb, "seek," occurs three times, but each time with a different object: "Seek the LORD"; "seek righteousness"; "seek humility."

The actual situation of the prophet's summons to his contem-

91

porary congregation is that it is Yahweh they have lost and it is
his will they have forgotten to follow! According to 1:17, where
we read "They have sinned against the Lord," the verb *hata'*
shows just wherein they have pursued the wrong goal; in so doing
they have lost Yahweh! This lost God must now be found! In like
manner Amos made his summons (Amos 5:5, 14) promising that
thereby they would find life. While for Amos life was something
one possessed, here in the judgment was the very condition of
possessing life. The word *tsedaqah* (RSV "righteousness") means
human behavior in a functional sense connected with the Covenant. It is something to be striven for, that which corresponds
with Yahweh's proclaimed will, what has been inscribed in the
document of the Covenant, the Decalogue. *'Anawah* means "humility," doing obeisance, paying homage. This is the very opposite of the presumptuousness, pride, and vanity of which the
prophet had accused his fellow citizens in their behavior. This
was Zephaniah's own particular view, yet one which agrees with
Isaiah's concept of what faith means. So it is a new religious and
moral behavior that is in question, corresponding to the prescriptions of the Covenant contract.

In Zephaniah's preaching the verb *shub* does not occur in the
sense of turning, of conversion. Yet this concept of conversion
with its distinguishing features is actually grappled with in quite
a pregnant form.

The prophet summons the self-centered, self-sufficient people
to take heed to themselves, to pull themselves together, to step
out of their stubbornness. "Let a man examine himself" (1 Cor.
11:28), let him acquaint himself with his situation, let him start
the journey toward God, who has already begun to move toward
him. In such self-knowledge and discovery of one's situation the
stage of losing one's goal becomes evident. Once this is recognized
one must not then remain merely aware of the true situation but
must in that situation do what is the will of God. Conversion is
not a change of mood, it is not being cheered up — it is a change
of one's whole frame of mind, a complete change of direction.
The self-centered, self-confident people must see that worship of
self plunges one into ruin. One must humble onself before God,
whom till now one had supposed to be impotent and incapable
of action (1:12). What one must do is to show evidence of loyalty
to the Covenant both in respect of God and of one's fellow human
beings, in conformity with the twin tablets of the Decalogue.

A conversion of this nature is the only protection, the only
shield and buckler in the coming "Day of Wrath." The word

tissateru points to Yahweh's mercy which can "hide" at the time of judgment. The final outcome is in Yahweh's hands; it is in his power to refrain even in the judgment! '*Ulay*, "perhaps," "it could be that" — thus it is a question of uncertainty, for in his actions the mighty LORD is free. He lives free in his love and works in the freedom of his love!

ANNOUNCEMENT OF JUDGMENT UPON FOREIGN NATIONS AND UPON JERUSALEM (2:4– 3:8)

In one long independent pericope we have a prophecy about foreign peoples; as a conclusion a judgment is repeated once again upon Jerusalem. It is clearly a unity in that a later redactor has collected prophecies he has obtained from various circles and then edited them. Many questions arise to which we cannot give decisive answers. Why does the prophet cite just these particular nations that are Judah's neighbors and proclaim judgment on them? Why does he not exemplify the judgment in each instance? Why is there no word about Phoenicia or Edom? Why such a short oracle on the Cherethites? We could answer these questions, handling them only from the prophet's theological stance, but then we would not be providing conclusive answers; thus these questions must remain open.

Following from the prophet's universal perspective is an announcement of the general judgment (1:2-3, 18) to take place on the Day of the LORD's Wrath. This decree oversteps the boundaries of the chosen people's land and spreads onto the foreign nations as well. Within this unified passage the concept of the *yom Yahweh* does not appear. But the predictions of the prophet, in the form of a verdict, which will come to pass in the future, without doubt are connected with the events of the Day of Wrath. As to this "day," no matter how much it will weigh upon the chosen people in the first place, no one at all will be able to extricate himself. The particle *ki* ("for") at v. 4 points to this. Since even the surrounding countries are to become desolate, it would be a useless exercise for God's people to seek for refuge in foreign lands (see Rudolph, p. 279). This theological view is supported and clarified also by the editorial form of the section, in that the oracles against the foreign nations are so placed beside each other that they cover the four points of the compass and thus express the universal judgment of the LORD upon the whole world. From Judah westward it reaches to Philistia (2:4-7); eastward to Moab and Ammon (2:8-11); southward to Cush (Ethiopia) (2:12); northward to Assyria (2:13-15). Five nations thus receive judgment in four paragraphs.

The final oracle is remarkable. In it the prophet not only gives reasons for the judgment but also deals in detail with the mighty Assyrians, pronouncing judgment upon Nineveh, their capital city. The prophet's own personal viewpoint is concealed here in relation to the events of his period. Assyria along with its capital city was still basking in the radiance of its might. The time period precedes the year 612, before the fall of Nineveh.

The contents of the section 2:4–3:8 may be divided into five parts:

1. Judgment upon Philistia, 2:4-7
2. Judgment upon Moab and Ammon, 2:8-11
3. Judgment upon Cush (Ethiopia, Egypt), 2:12
4. Judgment upon Assyria and Nineveh, 2:13-15
5. Woe to the rebellious city and its leaders, 3:1-8

Judgment upon Philistia (2:4-7)

Verses 4-7 are an oracle about the Philistines. The five cities of the Philistines were Gaza, Ashkelon, Ashdod, Ekron, and Gath. Here the prophet does not mention Gath. We may suppose that it goes unmentioned because in the period of the Assyrian invasion Gath was already laid waste, or it may have reverted to Judah (see Amos 1:6). Sennacherib handed over this territory in 701 to the Philistines, and it was only under the rule of Manasseh that it reverted once again. Or else it was absorbed into the territory of Ashdod and so fell under its suzerainty. The prophet gives no reasons for the judgment. Sufficient is the fact that they were living on the territory of the chosen people, on the promised land (see Rudolph, pp. 297-98). The cities are enumerated moving from south to north, and the judgment is expressed in word-plays that employ alliteration in the Hebrew. The feeling for this cannot be translated into other languages. The names are the direct expression of the judgment. They are "names pregnant with fate," as the German exegete Kühner (p. 31) puts it. Each bears the content of the oracle in two constituent forms: the announcement of the judgment embodied in the name (v. 4), and with it the concretizing of that judgment directed at the cities "clothed" in the LORD's own words (vv. 5-7).

The words ʿazzah ʿazubah tihyeh are composed in the form of a pun. Gaza shall be deserted—people will trample on Gaza. ʿAzab means desert, leave to its own devices, remain all alone. This means that the city will remain defenseless against its enemies and so become despoiled. *Ashkelon lishmamah* (note the alliteration) means Ashkelon will become a desolation, sterile and waste. *Ashdod yegareshuha:* Ashdod will be sacked along with its inhabitants. At noon, when, in that climate, people necessarily take a siesta, the enemy will storm into the city and drag off the population that will not know how to defend itself. In the next phrase we should again note the alliteration: *ʿEqron teʿaqer:* Ekron will be completely uprooted, the city being totally annihilated. Here again then we meet with wordplay.

The wording of the various judgments is contained in vv. 5-7. The prophet calls those Philistines who live along the seashore "you nation of the Cherethites." They had emigrated from the island of Crete. Thus the Philistines were not Semites in origin; they were originally from the southwest area of Asia Minor. They had stayed in Crete for a lengthy period and then settled in the land of Palestine in the time of Joshua. The people of Israel had fought bitter battles with them in the period of the Judges, in the beginning of the kingship, and chiefly during the reign of David. The fruitful seacoast, this people famous for their battle equipment in their well-strengthened cities, their fate was to be annihilation. The verb *ʾabad* includes such images as becoming ruined, being deprived, wiped out. These impregnable cities were to become heaps of ruins, their inhabitants exterminated. The prophecy points to this devastation in the words: "You, O seacoast, shall be pastures, shepherd's quarters, folds for flocks" (v. 6). Customarily the shepherding of sheep did not demand first-class grazing ground.

Verse 7 bears the mark of an editor writing during or after the Captivity. After the national catastrophe, that is, after the sequence of events that followed 587, he added his comments into this oracle, and in this way depicted before the eyes of the people in their time of trial a glorious future that would be prepared for them by Yahweh. In essence the prophet is pointing here to the mercy of God, who even in his judgments remains the merciful LORD, who is ever mindful of his Covenant and keeps it.

In the life of the chosen people, the *shab shabut* (RSV "restore fortune") formula expresses a significant event to follow, one that will emerge in the eschaton (3:19). It will reverse their fate and restore to the people their original state. Here appears for the first time in the prophet's theology the very significant concept of the "Remnant." This word was a sign that as a people they had met with grace. Out of his sovereign love Yahweh had gone beyond the judgment and was allowing them to share in his free gift of salvation that had been prepared for those who did not deserve it. What we have is a picture of a flock in the "time of salvation" that is peacefully grazing. The expression implies security, tranquility; it gives a masterly revelation of a life of joy lived without fear (see below on 3:14-20). The verb *paqad* (RSV "be mindful") here opens our eyes not to Yahweh's punishment but to his compassion. The Proprietor concerns himself with the fate of his tenants, and provides them with a secure, safe, and delightful dwelling place. Such are the essential requirements of an untroubled life.

Judgment upon Moab and Ammon (2:8-11)

It is significant that in this prophecy it is Yahweh who is speaking, calling himself "the God of Israel" and "the LORD of hosts." His oath by himself, "as I live" (v. 9), gives a special emphasis to his words.

Judah's two eastern neighbors were Ammon on the east bank of the Jordan River, alongside the tribe of Gad, and Moab a little to the south, on the eastern shore of the Dead Sea, alongside the tribe of Reuben. The two nations regarded themselves as related, as descended from Lot (Gen. 19:30-38). When the chosen people met up with them at the time of the conquest (Deut. 2:9, 19), they entered into conflict. The Balaam stories have something to say about that (Num. 22–24). We learn of their various antagonisms and quarrels about boundaries from the period of the Judges (Judg. 3:12ff.; 10:7-17), and in the time of Saul and David (1 Sam. 11:11, 14-17; 2 Sam. 8:2ff.; 10:11ff.; 12:26). In the story of the division of the kingdom these peoples acted with enmity (2 Kgs. 1:1; 3:4; 13:20). Yet we find them also practicing good neighborly relationships (1 Sam. 22:3; Ruth 1; 2 Sam. 10:2).

Since Yahweh entitles himself "God of Israel," he reveals that when hurt touches his people, it touches him too. Thus the judgment cannot be dispensed with. God punishes his own people because of their sins, but he does not permit that punishment to injure their foreign neighbors. God reserves all judgment to himself, for he always keeps in view his alliance with his chosen people whom he criticizes. His judgment is justified when seen from this point of view.

A double indictment extends to Moab and Ammon because of their double sin. The one is their taunting and reviling with which they abused the chosen people. *Herpah* means scoffing, holding in contempt, taunting. *Gidduph* means decrying, vilifying. The prophet does not describe this in so many terms; rather he points to the inner disposition, to their conceit and pride (v. 8), as the basic reason for their behavior. This disposition was the cause of their second sin, their territorial expansion at the expense of the covenant people. The emphasis here is that these neighbors have injured the integrity of the promised land, the inheritance of the covenant people (see Amos 1:13; Isa. 16:6, 25; Jer. 48:29ff.; 2 Kgs. 24:2; 27:3; 40:11). The prophet is thus giving a theological interpretation to historical facts.

The judgment here, as in the oracle on the Philistines, is one of devastation and barrenness. The brother nation is under the same judgment, descended as they are from the same original father, Lot, whose hometown, Sodom, had been destroyed (Gen. 19), along with those neighboring towns on the shores of the Dead Sea (Deut. 29:23). *Harul* means any wild weeds, such as nettles or brushwood, thus giving a picture of desolation. *Mikreh melah* were salt pits, another expression suggesting barrenness and desolation.

As in v. 7 here again the idea of a "remnant" appears. Even here too Yahweh maintains in grace the people he has judged! The LORD of the Covenant gives them back as their inheritance this stolen territory. The editor writing after the Exile is witness to this.

In this his general judgment Yahweh calls in question the power of all strange divinities. The prophet proclaims the LORD's uniqueness and absolute might, declaring that God will "famish" *(razah)* the gods, wasting them and annihilating them. This very helplessness will become the driving power that will lead the peoples to the one true and eternal God. The verb *shatah* ("bow down") conveys a declaration of allegiance, of worship. The nations, each in their own place, will thus worship and serve the LORD (see Isa. 2:2ff.; Zech. 14:16ff.; Mal. 1:11; John 4:24). Here too the prophet's universalist view shows itself.

Judgment upon Cush (Ethiopia, Egypt) (2:12)

The prophecy against the Ethiopians has survived only as a fragment; consequently it is the prophet's shortest oracle. This judgment has nothing to say about the land or other nations' territories; it is only about people—armies and soldiers. Nor is any explanation given of the provenance of the judgment. The prophet deals with only one issue, "the Ethiopians shall be slain by my sword."

This verse is understandable from the political events of the prophet's time. At that period Egypt had separated itself from its southern neighbor, Ethiopia. In this way there ended the reign of the Ethiopian dynasty that had ruled in Egypt over a long period (664-610). The prophet makes use of the ancient name *kushim*, "Cushites" (RSV "Ethiopians"), though actually this prophecy refers to Egypt. The Chronicles of Nabopolassar (see Rudolph, p. 282) tell how Egypt had kept observing the continual weakening of its old enemy, the Assyrians, ever since 616, and at the same time also the rising power of Babylonia. It tells of how they continually sent armed help along the coastal strip of land, thinking that it would be better to agree with their rivals than to confront the fearful armed might of Media and Babel. It was to these battalions sent to help these eastern armies that the judgment refers: "They will be the pierced ones of my sword" (so MT). This means that they will never again return to their homes. They will perish on the way, after their potential for war has proved to be without result. In this prophecy too appears Zephaniah's anti-Assyrian feeling, which stems from all the destruction they have wreaked on Judah and Jerusalem's cultic, social, and ethical life. This prophecy precedes the fall of Assyria and Nineveh, revealing that no human efforts could help them once the Lord of history had pronounced his judgment. Nineveh in fact fell in 612. The Assyrian host was then scattered and fled to Haran, where they sought to reorganize their army; but despite the help of Pharaoh Neco II (at Megiddo in 609), they finally succumbed in the battle of Carchemish in 605.

Judgment upon Assyria and Nineveh (2:13-15)

This prediction against Assyria and its capital city discloses the most detailed and also the hardest of judgments. One perceives that the prophet is now judging the real enemy, under whom the chosen people have suffered so much. In the form of a narrative the prophet imparts each one of God's judgments of destruction. Verse 13 exemplifies the Lord's judgment as he stretches out his hand (see v. 4) to judge Judah's northern neighbor. The *waw* consecutive imperfect of the verb *natan* means to open out, stretch out; *'abad* means to be lost, go to ruin, perish. Rudolph suggests that here we have a wish of the prophet — he expresses his longing for God's intervention. If only Yahweh would stretch out his hand, and if only he would lay waste Assyria! The judgment has reference to the whole land along with its capital city.

The striking picture of devastation in v. 14 portrays the judgment. The prophet never declares whether it is a question of a natural catastrophe or the result of enemy action. Nineveh was famous for its lofty buildings and for the strength of its walls. As well it was truly legendary for its palaces, gardens, and parks. Clearly the prophet was acquainted with all this. Assyria fell in its golden age, which were its last years. The destruction of the vegetation is pictured by the term *tsiyyah*. This word speaks of dry countryside and of steppe land. *Shemamah* covers the idea of wasteland and of bleakness; *midbar* means barrenness, without any life.

This city that had been inhabited for several centuries was now empty of inhabitants, and had become a mere fold for animals. The *qaʾat* was a bird of the desert; so owls had found a home among the ruins, within what window frames were still remaining. *Yeshorer*, the hooting of an owl, was a dreadful, alarming sound.

The above section of verse is written in the *Qinah* measure, the form employed in laments for the dead. This means that a deadly danger pulverizes the whole realm, including the capital city, and can result only in final devastation. This is truly the situation of which the prophet Nahum spoke: "There is no assuaging your hurt, your wound is incurable" (3:19). By the final destruction the prophet is not referring simply to an historical event but to the fact that behind the event stands the LORD, and he is Lord of all history.

Verse 15 gives the reason for the judgment. It is because of their presumption, self-worship, frivolous lifestyle, and false sense of security. In potential lunacy they had conceived the idea of their own glorious self-divination: *ʾani weʾaphsi ʿod* — "I am, and apart from me there is no one else!" Self-worship has no greater form, *non plus ultra*, than this, where the self-control of a sober mind can no longer control frayed nerves, owing to the demoralization of a person's whole self-conscious being. This then is to be the fate of the city as it lives the good life, *la dolce vita*, all in a false sense of security.

The horror and grisly nature of the judgment is graphically depicted. Whoever traverses, *ʿabar*, this countryside as a traveler will howl at this abomination, *sharaq*, will hiss, will whistle from repugnance as he sniggeringly utters words of spiteful glee. The verb *nuaʿ* means shake, tap, clap. It expresses in one dumbfounded moment a human gesture, as one acquiesces or expresses his helplessness in horror by clapping his hands together. Or it can describe a shout of malignant joy.

99

Woe to the Rebellious City and Its Leaders (3:1-8)

The series of prophecies against foreign nations is concluded by a judgment upon Jerusalem and its government. This is a threatening indictment by the prophet as he lays bare the sins of Jerusalem and declares that its leaders are responsible for its ruins (vv. 1-5). After this speech by the prophet there follows the Word of Yahweh himself. It has universal validity with respect to his acts of judgment, at the same time formulating the future with his acts of grace (vv. 6-8). These last verses may therefore be regarded as a bridge to the prophet's promises of salvation, linking this section to the eschatological section in the second half of ch. 3 (vv. 9-20).

In vv. 1-5, Jerusalem, the holy city, along with its leaders, is once again seated on the prisoners' bench (see 1:4-6, 8-9). Once again the cry for the dead, *hoy!* (see 2:5), leads off the words of the prophecy, indicating that in the prophet's eyes Jerusalem is Zion's centerpiece because of the number of its deadly sins! (v. 1). After this generalization the prophet lists those concrete sins that have justified the destruction (v. 2). He indicates the corrupt officials who have brought about the fall of the city (vv. 3-4). After this follows Yahweh's listing of his own activities, his judgment and his pardon (vv. 5-8), bearing witness that he is the LORD who acts.

The city is never expressly named, yet from the disclosure in v. 1 it is clear that only Jerusalem can be meant; the Syriac and the Targum versions can be disregarded when they suppose the reference is to Nineveh. Three signs expose the sins of the holy city, all three being participles. She is (1) *mor'ah*, rebellious, mutinous, disobedient, from the Qal feminine active participle of the root *mr'*. She is (2) *nig'alah*, defiled, bloodstained, unclean. The verb *ga'al* is one of the key expressions of the OT, where in its first form it means "redeem." But its second meaning, in the Niphal, Piel, Pual, Hiphil, and Hithpael, especially in the later writings (e.g., Isa. 59:3; 63:3; Mal. 1:7, 12; Ezra 2:62; Neh. 7:64; Dan. 1:8), refers to being bloodstained, unclean in the cultic sense, filthy. She is (3) *yonah*, repressive, bullying, crushing. So these are the signs of the contrast with that of Jerusalem, the city of David, the holy city, the dwelling place of the LORD of the Covenant. The center, the very heart of the life of the covenant people has come to this! God's holiness demands ethical behavior arising from a sanctified way of life in every sphere!

Jerusalem's "signs" point to the three directions of its actual

sins and to mortal man's threefold relationship to his environment — to God, to the cult, to his fellow human beings. It is a
question here of the mode of his behavior, since his ethical conduct arises from a true knowledge of Yahweh. A right knowledge
of God has but the one source in true divine worship, and it is
the exclusive norm for man's ethical conduct. By this means the
prophet reveals the religious, cultic, and socio-ethical collapse in
Jerusalem. Zephaniah denounces their studied perversity against
Yahweh's declaration, against the source of the true knowledge
of God, and expresses this concretely in four respects: (a) she
"listens to" *(shema')* no voice; (b) she "accepts" *(laqah)* no correction (the LXX has *paideia*); (c) she does not trust, *batah;* (d) she
does not draw near *(qarab)* to her God. The issue here is the
judgment upon her studied behavior. Israel's God, the LORD of
the Covenant, the living God, the God who speaks, who expresses
himself in his Word, is he who shapes and raises up for himself
his covenant people. Knowledge of God in this sense is an event,
because it is the result of Yahweh's acts.

But Jerusalem, rebellious and defiled, is not able to grasp
God's revelatory work, nor does she submit to his "pedagogy."
Completely missing here is any childlike trust *(batah);* rather she
had trusted in herself and her material goods (1:6, 12), for she
had estranged herself from her God. These four negative expressions of behavior are implict in man's natural negative response
to the cult and to human society. It was because of this that
Jerusalem, the capital city, had become rebellious *(mor'ah)*. She
had resisted revelation and thrust it from her. In the place where
the holy LORD dwelt, in the temple itself, she had practiced a
strange cult in the manner of the paganism around her. The
desired cultic purity was a mere show; the practices of a faithless
priesthood had actually become disgusting in the eyes of the people. According to the prophet's socio-ethical critique, in the city
oppression *(yonah)* was rampant; the officials were bullies, ex-
ploiting and fleecing the lower classes. The prophet was thus
laying bare the heinous sins that produced a corrupt situation.

According to vv. 3-4 the responsibility lay with her officials,
who were not fulfilling their obligations. They were abusing their
positions as public servants by imposing their own authority,
misusing the honor of their office. It was these people who, on
the basis of their calling, should have taught the covenant people
how to exercise God's "pedagogy" and make it relevant; and so
they were seriously negligent. They turned their whole service to
their own advantage, and in establishing it for their private gain

demeaned it. In truth these were mortal servants of a dying Jerusalem. Default of office and abuse of their position resulted in
a deathly collapse; they themselves had become as the living dead.
It was they who were the rebels (v. 4b), filthy (v. 4a), violent men
(vv. 3, 4c).

The prophet directs accusations against four strata among the
officials, and in so doing he preaches a sermon that is very much
to the point. He gives a description of the officials, judges, prophets, and priests. This becomes an exhibition of their sins that
bring about the inevitable collapse. "The political governors are
pitiless, the judges are vampires, the prophets are frivolous, the
priests are blasphemers" is the terse description made by the
Hungarian scholar Kecskeméthy. The government officials, *sarim,*
and the judges, *shophetim,* are depicted in horrific language: the
leaders are like roaring lions, the judges like desert wolves. These
pictures show the cruelty, the greed, the insatiable appetite, along
with the continual danger to life and limb; this passage speaks
of a condition of strain from never-ending terror that gripped
people like a slow-acting deadly poison. The top officials and
judges, whose task it actually was to see to the good of the lower
classes and to guarantee their security, worked through the use
of terror. They expropriated wrongly the goods of others and kept
in fear those committed to their care. Power had become demonic
in their hands; they knew no forbearance. A lust for profiteering,
a whetting of the appetite for private gain defined their lifestyle.
A roaring lion, inciting terror and fear, expressed how defenseless
people viewed their governors; desert wolves swift for their prey,
hurriedly devouring everything with insatiable greed. Such pictures occur often in the prophets (Mic. 3:1ff.; 7:4; Jer. 2:8; 5:31;
21:21-23; Ezek. 22:23-31).

The sins of the prophets and priests are not quite so brutal;
yet while of a more spiritual character, they resulted all the more
in severe and deep hurt. These more psychological sins Zephaniah traces back to abuse of office and to a paling of a sense of
vocation or even to its dying out. As to the prophets, he mentions
a twofold sin connected with a twofold form of faithless service —
he describes personal relationships in terms of service. *Pohazim*
means braggarts, liars, boasters, blusterers, "bigmouthed" persons. They did not take their office seriously, but accommodating
themselves to the mood of the day they misrepresented the Word
of God. They sought to make it more palatable and popular in
the hope of earning more cash. They refined this Word to the
point of deception, a very dangerous thing to do. The prophets

had prostituted it; they became involved in a deceitful jugglery that betrayed the Word entrusted to them. Yahweh's own speech had become the mouthpiece of human thoughts. This was a sure sign that their sense of calling had died out. The prophets no longer felt any responsibility toward the *dabar*, the Word; they were no longer capable of grasping it and speaking it forth, unadulterated, to the worshiping community. Another sign was that they were '*anshe begodot*, faithless men (RSV), who were now rebels, who could not care less about their calling and so exploited their position. The verb *bagad* points straight away to their instinctive disposition toward corruption in the performance of their activities.

The priests too earn a twofold charge: they profane what is sacred, and do violence to the Torah. The charge was *hillelu qodesh*, meaning that they "unhallowed" the holy. The priest was the guardian of the holy in the cult, first of all at the holy place, and then in the everyday life of the cultic community. In practice this refers to the daily sacrifice and to the holding of the annual Day of Atonement (Lev. 8:16; 21:1-24). The priest was called to serve the will of Yahweh exclusively: "You shall be holy, for I the LORD your God am holy" (Lev. 19:2). This charge could apply to the abundance of sins performed at the holy place, in the first instance in the abuse of the sacrifices in connection with their presentation, and in the profanation of the holy things. According to the prophet Ezekiel (22:26) such profanation did indeed take place when the priest saw no difference between the sacred and the profane, between the clean and the unclean, and when they "disregarded my sabbaths." Here the prophet points to the insensibility of "enlightened" priests, in whose view, because of their hardened and indifferent hearts, the boundaries between the holy and the profane had become effaced. The charge raises the question of whether the priests' priestly status and service could be upheld. Was there any need for such priestly service that completely lacked any signs of the characteristic service of Yahweh? Did such a priest have any right to serve at all when he abused his calling in this way?

The priest was not only the guardian of the holy, he was also the guardian of the Torah. The priest "dispensed Torah," that is, he communicated to the worshiping community the will of Yahweh and taught them how to keep to it (cf. Hos. 4:6; Jer. 2:8). Instead of doing so they did "violence [*hamas*] to the law" (RSV), interpreting it arbitrarily. They inserted into their interpretation their

103

own ideas, made to fit the popular desires. In this way they were conveniently silent about the whole truth of it and made it fit their own interests.

According to Zephaniah's critique, both the priests and the prophets had become faithless stewards. They had been handling the task committed to them in a conscienceless manner, and so had brought about the collapse of the covenant people. If the blind leads the sightless, then naturally both will fall into a pit (Matt. 15:14). In this way, because of her faithless leaders, the holy city has plumbed hopeless depths. Deservedly Zephaniah sings over her a lament for the dead.

After such an unveiling and display of all the sins of the charismatics, it comes as a surprise not to hear an announcement of judgment in v. 5. The unveiling done in this manner is in itself the judgment upon the charismatics. Following upon the above verses, v. 5 opens up a striking conclusion: the charismatics are not in their place, yet despite that Yahweh is present! There he stands in the midst of her, "within her" (RSV) as the righteous *(tsaddiq)* and compassionate God. To be sure, God does not identify himself with his corrupt people, "he does no wrong," ʿ*awlah,* but he does not leave them to themselves. Despite their faithless handling of the Torah in the holy place, Yahweh's concern is that his *mishpat,* his judicial sentence, should be effective in all circumstances. "From morning to morning he brings it to light," or, more accurately, "practices" what the leaders of the cultic community fail to do. Within the city, sick unto death, in spite of everything, there is present the living LORD in action! Within Jerusalem, where only faithlessness, deceit, cheating, and repression exist, there God administers righteousness and justice. It is only this expensive medicine that can cure the cultic and socioethical life that is in decay. Yahweh himself takes in hand his people's affairs at that point where the faithless charismatics have created deadly danger, and by his gracious work heals the deadly wounds they have left.

Verses 6-8 employ an independent tapestry, which belongs to the genre that describes the threats and rebukes through which Yahweh speaks. Jerusalem is addressed (v. 7a). The LORD appears in the form of a judge and accuses her on the basis of her undeniable deeds (v. 8). The same motif is apparent as has occurred already at 1:18 — Yahweh in the fire of his jealous love will consume the whole world. Clearly this is an insertion by the same editor.

In v. 6 God turns Jerusalem's attention upon the events of world history with a teaching purpose. If she is indeed so exceedingly hardened that the very presence of the LORD in Jerusalem has aroused in her no reverence or fear to keep her from trespassing, look at Yahweh's might in his judgment upon the nations of the world, and pay heed! The word "battlements," *pinnot,* speaks of strength, of bastions, but indicates that before God what should have been unconquerable are a mere nothing. The wasted streets, the ruined cities, the uninhabitable areas, these point to the seriousness of the judgment and proclaim the might of God. The turbulent history of the Near East is a dramatic example of this.

According to v. 7 Israel had not learned from these examples, although her God had thought that with all these instructive examples before her, with all their various outcomes, she would fear him, *yare',* would accept the pedagogical means used for her instruction, *musar,* and so would escape the judgment due her for her sins.

The verb *paqad,* punish (RSV "enjoined"), here also expresses the mighty calling to account when the prophet surveys their homeland and sees that they deserve their punishment. Not only did Israel refuse to learn from the events of world history, and in consequence did not bow before her LORD; she had actually bit by bit multiplied her sins. As soon as she awoke, so soon as she found opportunity to offend, she had already acted and in this way provoked the punitive wrath of Yahweh.

[The author's Hungarian Bible reads at v. 7a: "I thought that she would surely fear me, and would accept the hint; then her dwelling place would not be destroyed, even as I had not wanted to punish her." This is in close conformity with the Hebrew.]

Thus it is understandable that the threat should become all the more acute, for the censure passes over into an actual announcement of judgment: "Therefore wait for me!" Certainly there is no escaping the judgment! Yahweh now stands forth as witness and makes his accusations on the basis of undeniable facts. The designated day, the Day of Wrath, is the time of the final reckoning (cf. 1:15; 2:2). This means a new turn of events. Alongside Judah's judgment will be the disclosure of the judgment upon the peoples. It will be an expression of judgment repeated universally. It is similar to the preamble to the judgment at 1:18, which speaks of Yahweh's jealous love — *'esh qin'ati,* his passion to protect the Covenant.

PROPHECIES OF UNIVERSAL SALVATION (3:9-20)

At v. 9 there begins, in the last part of the last chapter of Zephaniah's book, a series of promises of salvation by Yahweh. It is to be noted that this announcement of universal salvation is addressed both to Judah and to the pagan peoples. The universal author of this redemption is Yahweh. The prophet proclaims this to the people with particular emphasis to those inhabitants of Judah and Jerusalem who had taken the view that God does nothing, either good or evil (1:12).

Verses 14-20 contain the prophet's eschatology. This concerns that time of salvation when the fate of the chosen people will radically change. That decisive change will take place through acts of Yahweh when his relationships with the nations will be on the same plane as with the people of the LORD. What we have here is the transformation to a new way of life, the sign of which will be true divine worship and service of Yahweh (v. 9).

The section 3:9-20 is not of one piece. Noticeable here is the handiwork of the redactor who has collected the prophecies and edited them as one work. We can find in it the motif of Yahweh's ascension of the throne (Elliger). Here also one may observe features characteristic of exilic and postexilic eschatology: the LORD calling his enemies to account, the reassembling of his scattered people, and his returning them to their own land to glorify God before the eyes of the foreign nations. This section employs anthropomorphic images to depict the God who acts — he is judge, army commander, bridegroom, shepherd (vv. 15, 17, 19).

The pericope may be divided into three parts according to its contents:
1. The LORD's promise, vv. 9-13
2. Zion's joy: "The LORD is in your midst," vv. 14-17
3. Realization of the day of grace, vv. 18-20

The LORD's Promise (3:9-13)

These verses may be classified in terms of a prophetic promise of salvation. Yahweh himself speaks, addressing Judah and the pagan peoples. At the center of the prophecy stands the act of Yahweh. There is no report of a judge pronouncing sentence upon their deeds; what we have is an announcement about certain re-creative acts on the part of the God of grace. These acts are astonishing and extraordinary.

Verse 9 points to an act such as could result only from a radical change. This is expressed by the verb *haphak*, turn, turn right round, turn away, be transformed, collapse, sink out of sight, totally change. All these terms express the idea that it is not a gradual, consistent, developing change that is meant, but the result of a sudden, vigorous interference. Such a radical change took place in Saul's life, when "God changed his heart," *leb*, the center of one's life (1 Sam. 10:9), or, with the RSV, "God gave him another heart." Thus he became a completely different man to the extent that those who saw him asked: "What has come over the son of Kish?" In the same way the cities of Sodom and Gomorrah perished, sank out of sight into the nearby Dead Sea at God's rigorous judgment (Gen. 19:21, 25, 29; Deut. 29:33). In Hos. 11:9 the same verb portrays the great and ultimate "change" that takes place in God's heart when he executes his justice in such a way that he does not bring about punishment upon faithless Israel, his thankless children, but takes it upon himself and bears it himself. This verse pictures God as anguished, as struggling inwardly with himself. It reveals what results from the final victory of his love through that "decisive change." Instead of the death of his faithless people, he leads them to life.

This decisive act of Yahweh, this radical "change," has to do with the pagan nations, the *ʿammim*. Some scholars would alter that word to *ʿammi*, meaning "my people," with reference to Israel alone. But to do so would limit Zephaniah's universal eschatological perspective. The word *kullam*, meaning all, everyone, does not support this view.

The words *saphah berurah*, "pure speech" (RSV), imply lips that have been purified, set apart, lips that have been singled out. This is the opposite of the expression *temeʾ sephatayim* found at Isa. 6:5, where the prophet's self-consciousness occasions in him a fear of death: "I am a man of unclean lips." Here the word "lips" refers not just to one particular instrument of human speech, but expresses implicitly the instrument that reveals the inner ego. This understanding of the word is supported by the verb *haphak*, whose use indicates a decisive change in the depths of the inner person. This is a miracle in the directing of the human heart that remains a secret, in that it is one aspect of God's re-creative work. It becomes clear from the interdependence of this text and the whole prophecy that strange cultic activities and the worship of foreign gods contaminate the very existence of the whole person. Thus even his lips are rendered unclean. The purpose of Yahweh's action is to appeal to the nations to call on his name — *liqroʾ beshem Yahweh*.

The object of God's action is the bringing into being of true worship. As the realization of his creative purpose, the Creator establishes man's worship and service, for it is to God that man owes his very life. This expression unites the summons to call upon his name with the motif to witness to it. According to the cultic community's natural rhythm of life, they are not only to invoke but also to proclaim the name of God. Divine worship is to proceed not only within the limits of the cult but in every area of human life. The verb *'abad* points to this, that a lifestyle lived according to the will of God means service of him in every area of life.

The unification of faith and witness is shown moreover in that people are to stand "shoulder to shoulder" (as we would say; actually, in Hebrew, "with one shoulder"), thus fulfilling Yahweh's will. This is expressed in the RSV by the phrase "with one accord." This picture of a common sharing of a burden between men and nations is a masterly illustration of and witness to a community taking shape. Rudolph sees a promise of world peace in it. The prophet Isaiah's characteristic eschatological features are emphasized in it — the nations will flow to Zion's hill and will beat their swords into ploughshares and their spears into pruning hooks; and "nation shall not lift up sword against nation, neither shall they learn war any more" (Isa. 2:4).

Verse 10 speaks of the spread of the worship of God. From far in the south, which in those days people took to be the end of the earth, will come Yahweh's suppliants bringing their offerings with them. Here we are not just to think of the gathering in of all Jews of the diaspora; rather, on the basis of his universal vision the prophet is referring to all the world's peoples, of whom the Ethiopians of the far south represent the people who stand at the farthest distance from Israel. "The daughter of my dispersed ones" refers to the masses of pagan peoples as a counterpart to the name "daughter of Zion," which is applied to the chosen people (3:14). "My offering," *minhah*, was a voluntary addition to the regular sacrifice as an expression of gratitude and respect. It had to do with the communal feast connected with the sacrifice. Yahweh, now reconciled, takes part in it unseen. He undertakes to be in communion with his people at the festive meal following the performance of the sacrifice.

The radical transformation meant a complete break with the old life, in that Yahweh had completed a total cleansing (v. 11). The effect of Yahweh's deeds was the establishment of a new situation that was just the reverse of what the prophet had pronounced judgment upon in his own day. The root of the people's sin against the LORD had been rebellion, *pesha͑*, concrete expression of which was their pride, *ga᾽awah*, and haughtiness, *gabehah*, their belief in their own importance. No kind of self-conceit will any longer befoul Yahweh's holy hill, his dwelling place, and nothing will spoil the people's worship of God. In this way Yahweh's universal rule will be realized.

Since he will remove, *sur*, from his holy hill all "your proudly exultant ones," he will leave, *᾽asir*, in the new aeon a new people, the Remnant (v. 12). This concept was already present a century earlier in the preaching of Amos and Isaiah (Amos 5:15; Isa. 10:20-21), in connection with Yahweh's acts of liberation. Conjoined in Zephaniah's theology are the Remnant, the new creation, and the work of the Redeemer and Savior God, who opens up a future for his people and presents them with a whole new lifestyle.

The prophet stresses three marks of this lifestyle: (1) It is *῾ani*, humble and lowly, a mark of those who submit to the will of Yahweh and obey him. In this connection 2:2b has shown the conditions of the liberation indicated. (2) Another mark is the word *dal*, weak, insignificant, powerless, needy. Both of these concepts belong in the realm of social ethics, and this is pushed vigorously in the prophet's preaching. *Dal* speaks of a situation where people are deprived of their legal rights, are held in contempt and exploited by their neighboring rich or by the powers that rule them (Amos 8:4; Isa. 3:14, 15; 10:2, 30; etc.; Hab. 3:14). It appears repeatedly in the Book of the Covenant (Exod. 20 – 22), and we find it in the prescriptions of Deuteronomy (15:11). Yet Zephaniah does not make use of these two marks in a sociological sense but in an expressly theological one. He handles them in their relation to Yahweh, as the mode of the new behavior pattern required in the new lifestyle. In his interpretation of this passage Rudolph emphasizes the subjective element in this concept. We are dealing with people who feel themselves helpless and insignificant in the sight of God. Such conduct is the very opposite of the haughtiness, the pride, the self-satisfied indifference which the prophet had so loudly denounced in his contemporaries (1:6, 12; 2:10, 15; 3:11). The Remnant, "those who are left," are aware of their littleness and powerlessness impelling them to depend upon the mighty LORD, to whom they flee for refuge, there to find shelter. (3) The third mark is just this, that they trust in the name of the LORD, *hasu beshem Yahweh*. They will hide themselves in the name of the LORD, in him they will seek refuge, and recognize that he is the only protection for their personal existence.

Yahweh is that "covering" where alone among the contingencies of life there is sure defense. This then is the new lifestyle of the newly created "Remnant."

Verse 13 is to be regarded as a later gloss, emphasizing the contents of the preceding verse. The distinctiveness of the new lifestyle is depicted as one that is totally removed from the corruptive leaven in its relations with God and one's fellow human beings—doing no wrong, uttering no lies, using no deceitful speech. *'Awlah* means perversity, crookedness, iniquity (Isa. 61:8; 28:15; Hos. 10:9; Mic. 3:10; Hab. 2:12; Mal. 2:6); it sums up all the distortion apparent in the life of the chosen people in the prophet's time with respect to their religious, ethical, and social relationships. Using the Decalogue as his norm, from which he makes his disclosure, this picture evolves—one of *kazab,* lying, deceit, cheating; *tarmit,* intrigue, fraud, treachery. A tongue cleansed for divine worship excludes such speech, for by it community relationships are shattered when people purpose to mislead their neighbors and defraud them. This refers back to v. 9, where we have a masterly sketch of religious and community life.

This lifestyle means peace and security for the "Remnant." It is portrayed in a picture of pastoral life: "They shall pasture and lie down, and none shall make them afraid." Nourishment, tranquility, and protection are basic requirements in human life, its ultimate values and indispensable conditions.

Zion's Joy: "The LORD Is in Your Midst" (3:14-17)

The two following sections, vv. 14-17 and vv. 18-20, reveal the future of the chosen people, the time of salvation which the God of the Covenant has prepared for his people. Noticeable is the first song that the prophet intones as he bids people rejoice. Some scholars regard vv. 14-15 as part of a hymn that was sung as Yahweh ascended his throne. If we approach these verses with this in mind, then we are to regard them as speaking of the periodic succession of Yahweh's rule. But in its relationship to the rest of the prophecy just the opposite view emerges. God is present in every situation in the midst of his people. He "exercises" his *mishpat* methodically, regularly—"from morning to morning he shows forth his justice" (3:5). This means that Yahweh ceaselessly, without any break, rules in the fulfillment of his justice. Actually, in his justice he dispenses the outcome of his grace, that is, his creation of the new life. Thus it is not a question of Yahweh becoming king once again in the midst of his people; it is the demonstration of his royal power through his recreative acts by means of which he renders his rule evident before his covenant people. The whole atmosphere of the new age is one of joy.

Without any special introduction the prophet plunges *in medias res* into his prophecy of salvation (v. 14). He summons man in his whole being, *kol leb,* to be filled with an exultation that gushes forth jubilantly out of him. *Ranan* means to shout aloud, to exult, to be verdant, to flower; *rua'* means to yell, shout, roar, sound a trumpet; *sameah* means to shout with joy, dance, clap the hands, rejoice in exultation; *'alaz* is to be glad, delighted, make merry. These four terms for joy enlighten one another each from their own angle and reveal that great joy which people experience when their hearts are filled to overflowing. One does not rejoice at merely being told to do so without any special reason. The prophet is summoning the whole person to be full of exultation by point-ing to its real cause and source. Zion's joy has only one cause: "Yahweh has done it."

The LORD who acts is portrayed in two anthropomorphic pic-tures. The one is that of a judge. He has "taken away," *sur,* com-pletely altered, has changed his sentence. He is not going to push to their conclusion the legally justifiable decisions he has made as Judge. He will set free the sinner. Here, however, it is not a question of inconsistency on his part; it is a question of God's sovereign decision. As a consequence of his compassionate love he reverses the sentence he has pronounced and sets free the sinner. Such is the evidence of Yahweh's re-creative power.

The second picture is that of a war lord who has marched into the field of battle and sent the enemy fleeing: *pinnah* means turn away, disperse, move elsewhere, lose all trace of. Such complete and swift disappearance is shown by the use of the Piel of the verb. These actions refer back to the section 3:9-13, where God stood forth in the midst of the peoples and declared a judgment that was final and complete. The prophet here bears witness to the victorious power of God's love. In every situation he can create something new, in every circumstance he can uphold his people. The inference of all this is — "The LORD is in your midst." This means that God himself has conquered all the opposition of those who kept him distant from his people. It was because of them he had brought charges and pronounced judgment through his prophet. These charges were their adherence to a foreign cult (1:5), their alienation from Yahweh (1:6), their indifference (1:12), shamelessness, refractoriness, rebelliousness (2:1; 3:1), including the sins of the faithless officials (1:8; 3:3-4). But now, right at the

111

holy place, in the city of David, the LORD of the Covenant is present with his people!

In this new situation the cult is purified, clean lips call upon the LORD for help and proclaim his great name; the proud humble themselves, all social ills are healed, and the people bow before their LORD with their whole heart. "You shall fear evil no more." In that close relationship every hurtful power will lose its fearful character and the people will have gained complete security.

The summons to rejoice is made to "Daughter of Zion, Israel, daughter of Jerusalem." These three synonyms are a summons to the chosen people, and so refer to Yahweh's covenant people. All three are titles of honor, and in all three there sounds forth the constructive task of God's congregation. In them we hear of their election, the bonds of the Covenant, and the concern with which he has borne his people throughout the course of history. "Daughter of Zion" and "Daughter of Jerusalem" are titles addressed to the newly created Israel. She who was once "defiled Zion" and "rebellious Jerusalem" (3:1) has become as it were the young bride, radiating purity. Thus it becomes evident that God's congregation has no value in herself and commands no merit. Her totally different position and the dignity arising therefrom stem from the reality that her LORD loves her in a special way, caring for her and creating her anew.

Verses 16-17 unfold before us how the Lord himself rejoices. He adopts his people's joy and rejoices together with them. So decisive is this event that has come to pass in Israel's midst that God himself, the author of joy, rejoices with those who now rejoice. Once again we meet with a decisive anthropomorphic picture, that of a bridegroom in love (cf. Isa. 62:5). With a heart overflowing with joy he keeps silence alongside his betrothed, because they understand each other even without any words. This is a moving way of describing true and undisturbed communion. The expressions used for Yahweh's joy are *sus/sis,* rejoice, feel merry; *gil,* exult; and *rinnah,* shouting with joy (see v. 14).

The new situation requires new forms of behavior (v. 16). "On that day," on the day when Yahweh has brought about salvation, it shall be said to Jerusalem: "Do not fear, O Zion, let not your hands grow weak." We are to note that this verse conveys, as an oracle uttered in the holy place, what a prophet or a priest would say. *Raphah* means to languish, be despondent, be exhausted. The verb describes exhaustion of both body and spirit, when a person can no longer stand on his feet because of exhaustion. It is because the LORD is present that there is now no place for tiredness or exhaustion; he has fought and won the victory as *gibbor,* as the life-giving deliverer, *yoshia*ʿ (v. 17). It is probable that v. 17 is a gloss originating from the Captivity or from a period after it. On the basis of the influence of the previous verses, the editor has here written down his own witness to the promised future.

Realization of the Day of Grace (3:18-20)

The prophet has written the concluding section partly in prose, partly in verse. It envisages the establishment of Zion and the ultimate fulfillment of salvation. This section is from the hand of the one who has edited the whole book.

The historical background is the destruction of Judah and Jerusalem, the trials of the Captivity, and the people's sad fate, of torment, dispersion, hopelessness. Verse 18 is particularly corrupt. Thus problems of interpretation arise. Verses 19-20 express the same theme in other words — the re-establishment of Zion and the formation of a new lifestyle. Verse 20 looks like a paraphrasing of v. 19. The characteristics typical of postexilic eschatology dominate and unify the text — victory over the enemy, the gathering together and the bringing home of the dispersed along with their exaltation; the reversal of the fate of the chosen people (2:7) comes as the ultimate consequence.

Verse 18 is difficult to interpret. Some scholars suggest that the verse is a commentary on the previous verses or on the following heading. Others, under the influence of the LXX, translate it by "as on a day of festival" (so RSV), and join it to the previous verse.

The afflictions of the Captivity are what provide this verse with its background and with a key to its interpretation. Since God is present in his might and in his love, he exults in "being in love" with his beloved, and "rejoices with thee in song"; he does not permit his people to mourn. Those who "sorrow during a festival" are living in a situation of diaspora, scattered sons and daughters who are removed far from the place of worship and so cannot take part in the communal worship of the congregation. In the Psalms too this is felt to be a sorrowful experience (Ps. 24:4; 42:3; 44:2; 63:3; 137). This reality heightens the dejection occasioned by distance; the irony of their circumstances becomes an ever heavier burden upon them. So this is a picture expressing despair and helplessness. Yahweh's compassion and fellow-feeling, his gracious fatherly love shows itself in that he intervenes, acts, and thus totally alters the situation that otherwise is without hope. [The author's rendering of the obscure Hebrew text is not

113

the same as that of the RSV. The latter notes the MT's obscurity in two footnotes.]

The central theme of vv. 19-20 is a listing of Yahweh's acts along with their consequence, which is the final establishment of Zion. Once again we meet with anthropomorphic pictures portraying the invincible Warrior and the Shepherd. The verb *'oseh* as an active participle (RSV "deal with") applies to the mighty LORD who acts and before whom it is not possible to withstand. He comes in triumph, destroys all his enemies, and "deals with all your oppressors." The shepherd searches out and gathers together *(qibbets)* his scattered flock; in doing so he places them in safety, cares for their destiny, and thus ensures their future.

In their tormented, hopeless situation, incapable of helping themselves or unsure of what action to take, he pictures a people hurt, lame, and desperately needing help. The verbal root of "lame," *tsl'*, expresses both the condition and the situation at the same time, as both subjective and objective reality. It speaks of helpless persons, unable to make any move of themselves, living in trying circumstances, now being wakened to life, set upon their feet, made to walk, set free. All these movements are incorporated in the verb *yasha'*, the OT expression that offers another aspect of the concept of redemption. It refers to help in both its outer and its inner aspects, to help in assembling oneself, and to help in being assembled. Israel's restoration exhibits both (cf. 3:4; 1 Kgs. 22:17; Mic. 4:6; Jer. 23:3; Ezek. 34:4). The picture of the shepherd occurs in all the prophetic preaching in the OT as well as in the poetry of the Psalms. It portrays the single reality that Yahweh maintains his people in life.

Yahweh's extraordinary deed rescues the outcasts from the hand of the enemy and brings them together. "I will give you a name, and make you famous among the nations." [This is closer to the Hebrew than the RSV.] The *shem*, name, is the bearer of the inner "I," its "stamp." It declares, expresses, and defines its bearer: *Nomen est omen* — "A name is a sign." A new name points to a new personality, a new being. Israel has become new because she has been created anew by her holy LORD! On the occasion of the binding of the Covenant, Israel had received a name that distinguished her completely — "a kingdom of priests, a holy nation" (Exod. 19:6; cf. 1 Pet. 2:9). It expresses the new position into which the people entered when they bound themselves by the Covenant. Deuteronomy expresses it thus: "The LORD desires that you should be his own possession . . . that he will set you high above all nations that he has made, in praise and in name and in honor, and that you shall be a people holy to the LORD your God" (Deut. 26:18-19).

The "honor," *tehillah,* in which the chosen people will stand is that which occurs when they turn toward the LORD in their sorrow; he will redeem them and in so doing will display his *kabod,* that outspreading of his might which he will render visible throughout all creation. Yahweh requires Israel to share in his redemptive deeds by showing forth the LORD's glory, which will be recognized all around.

Herein lies the significance of the word "renowned." It indicates one's name, one's unique existential being. "I will 'make' you renowned" is actually the verb *natan,* give, along with *shem,* a name. They are terms that have to do with acts of Yahweh.

The summation of Yahweh's acts are in the words *shubi 'et-shebutekem* (RSV "restore your fortunes") — I shall reverse your fate, that is, I shall turn your situation to your good. An unknown editor has inserted here his own witness to this emphasis upon the reality of events with the word *le'enekem* — "before your eyes." You are going both to see and to participate in what God has promised — *'amar Yahweh,* "says the Lord." Verily it is so; verily it shall be; everything will be fulfilled — because not man's but Yahweh's mouth has spoken!

BIBLIOGRAPHY

Albright, W. F. "The Psalm of Habakkuk." In *Studies in Old Testament Prophecy Presented to T. H. Robinson*. Ed. H. H. Rowley (Edinburgh: T. & T. Clark, 1950), 1-18.

Bentzen, A. *Introduction to the Old Testament*. 5th ed. (Copenhagen: Gad, 1959).

Bič, M. *Trois prophètes dans un temps de ténèbres: Sophonie — Nahoum — Habaquq* (Paris: 1968).

Craigie, P. C. *The Minor Prophets, II.* Daily Study Bible — Old Testament (Philadelphia: Westminster, 1985).

Duhm, B. *Das Buch Habakuk* (Tübingen: Mohr, 1906).

Eaton, J. H. *Obadiah, Nahum, Habakkuk and Zephaniah*. Torch Bible Commentary (London: SCM, 1961).

————. "The Origin and Meaning of Habakkuk 3," *Zeitschrift für die alttestamentliche Wissenschaft* 76 (1964) 144-71.

Elliger, K. *Das Buch der zwölf Propheten, II.* Das Alte Testament Deutsch. 6th ed. (Göttingen: Vandenhoeck & Ruprecht, 1967).

Fohrer, G. *Introduction to the Old Testament*. Trans. D. Green (Nashville: Abingdon, 1968).

————. *Die Propheten des Alten Testaments, II. Die Propheten des 7. Jahrhundert* (Gütersloh: 1974).

Gerleman, G. *Zephania textkritisch und literarisch untersucht* (Lund: Gleerup, 1942).

Humbert, P. *Problèmes du livre d'Habacuc* (Neuchâtel: Secrétariat de L'Université, 1944).

Hyatt, J. P. "The Date and Background of Zephaniah," *Journal of Near Eastern Studies* 7 (1948) 25-29.

Kaiser, O. *Introduction to the Old Testament*. Trans. J. Sturdy (Minneapolis: Augsburg, 1975).

Kecskeméthy, I. *Kommentár Mikáh és Cefanjah próféták könyveihez* (1914).

Keller, C. A and R. Vuilleumier. *Michée — Nahoum — Habacuc — Sophanie.* Commentaire de l'Ancien Testament (Neuchâtel: Delachaux et Niestlé, 1971).

Kühner, H. O. *Zephanja, Prophezei* (Zurich: 1943).

Lüthi, W. *Habakuk rechtet mit Gott* (Basel: 1940).

Rendtorff, R. *The Old Testament: An Introduction*. Trans. J. Bowden (Philadelphia: Fortress, 1986).

117

Rudolph, W. *Micah — Nahum — Habakkuk — Zephaniah*. Kommentar zum Alten Testament. 2nd ed. (Gütersloh: Mohn, 1975).

Sellin, E. *Das Zwölfprophetenbuch übersetz und erklärt*. Kommentar zum Alten Testament. 3rd ed. (Leipzig: Diechert, 1929-30).

Smend, R. *Die Entstehung des Alte Testament*. 2nd ed. (Stuttgart/Berlin/Köln/Mainz: Kohlhammer, 1981).

Smith, J. M. P., W. H. Ward, and J. A. Bewer. *A Critical and Exegetical Commentary on the Books of Micah, Zephaniah, Nahum, Habakkuk, Obadiah and Joel*. International Critical Commentary (Edinburgh: T. & T. Clark; New York: Scribner's, 1911).

Smith, L. P. and E. R. Lacheman, "The Authorship of Zephaniah," *Journal of Near Eastern Studies* 9 (1950) 137-42.

von Ungern-Sternberg, R. and H. Lamparter. *Der Tag des Gerichtes Gottes: Habakuk, Zephanjah, Jona, Nahum*. Botschaft des Alten Testaments (Stuttgart: Calwer, 1960; 2nd ed. 1975).

Van der Woude, A. S. *Habakuk — Zefanja*. De Prediking van het Oude Testament (Nijkerk: Callenbach, 1978).

Vischer, W. *Der Prophet Habakuk*. Biblische Studien 19 (Neukirchen: Verlag der Buchhandlung des Erziehungsvereins, 1958) (= *Le Prophète Habaquq*. Trans. A. Cavin [Geneva: Labor et Fides, 1959]).